IMAGES
of England

Burton upon Trent
Recollections

His reverence the Canon
Has lost that worried look
For a "CANNON" STOVE
is now installed
His simple (?) fare to cook.

IMAGES
of England

BURTON UPON TRENT
RECOLLECTIONS

Geoffrey Sowerby and Richard Farman

'He who has no regard for his ancestors
will have none for his posterity.'

(Edmund Burke 1729-97)

TEMPUS

It would be difficult to find a scene more evocative of the Burton that has gone for ever-smoking chimneys, the stacks of barrels, the busy little engine, it almost conjures up the brewery smells and the hammering of the coopers – all present in this 1920s scene at Allsopps, prior to the amalgamation with Ind Coope, whose premises appear in the background.

Frontispiece: A well-known local ironmongery, established in the nineteenth century and trading well into the twentieth, Lobbs of the High Street issued this delightful publicity postcard shortly before the First World War. If you were a discerning cook this was the ultimate way of practising Burton Corporation Gas Company's slogan: 'Meals cooked by gas, are hard to surpass.' One can only sigh for luckless domestics who probably had to cope with nearly as much clearing up and cleaning as with the old stove it replaced – at least if the Canon's menu is anything to go by.

First published 2002

Tempus Publishing Limited
The Mill, Brimscombe Port,
Stroud, Gloucestershire, GL5 2QG

ISBN 0 7524 2642 7

Typesetting and origination by Tempus Publishing Limited
Printed in Great Britain by Midway Colour Print, Wiltshire

Contents

Sadly, as this book reached the final stages of production, Geoff Sowerby died. I dedicate this book, the last of many on which we collaborated, to his memory. With his passing Burton has lost a dedicated local historian. His knowledge of the area and his good humour will be missed be many.

Richard Farman

A striking contrast to the previous image – for relaxation on a summer afternoon in Victorian and Edwardian times, boating was immensely popular. Put the picnic baskets on board and gently row until a suitable shady spot is reached and you have the idyllic setting for a delightful souvenir photograph, capturing nostalgia for a more leisurely era. One recalls Kenneth Grahame's opening chapter of *The Wind in the Willows* when Ratty and Mole spend their day on the river: 'Nothing seems really to matter, that's the charm of it.'

Introduction

Washington Irving (1783-1859), although an American, wrote many studies of English life. He gave shrewd advice to anyone seeking to discover an area and the character of its inhabitants. He must go forth into the country; he must visit villages and hamlets, he must visit castles, villas, halls, farm houses, cottages; he must wander through parks and gardens, along hedges and green lanes; he must loiter about country churches, attend wakes and fairs and other local festivals; and discover the people in all their conditions and all their habits and humours.'

All this remains as true today as when written well over 150 years ago. Irving wrote, of course, of his own period, omitting references to industries that were newly developing when he wrote. But even when investigating olden days while compiling our books, we still endeavour to visit the locations and sites of which we have archive material. In fact, many industrial premises and sites have been developed and then dramatically changed or even disappeared again between Irving's time and the present day (coal mining, quarrying, the brewing scene, for example). However, in spite of the enormous changes we find, we still try to discover people, as Irving advocated, who themselves, or whose families, can recall scenes we want to portray.

Often our task inevitably becomes one of further investigation through maps, documents, newspapers, prints and photographs, old books, letters and family albums, by which means we hope to rediscover the story of a location and the lives of its inhabitants.

This has been our aim when compiling *Recollections* and hopefully we have been able to record accounts of wide appeal involving local people and places.

Since publishing Burton's first pictorial history collection in 1983 we have produced six volumes covering Burton, East Staffordshire and South Derbyshire. We have used hundreds of images to place on record illustrated stories of events and social history in towns and villages alike, in times which have changed the local scene out of all recognition and at a pace ever increasing, even since we produced our first volume.

It has always been our aim to share our collections and research and this book will complete an archive of over 1,000 images from all around Burton and District, recalling lost views, forgotten occasions and sweeping changes in many aspects of daily life.

Geoffrey Sowerby and Richard Farman
Burton upon Trent, July 2002

UNITED KINGDOM
BAND·OF·HOPE·UNION
PATRON
HIS MAJESTY THE KING.

CERTIFICATE of MERIT

AWARDED TO

Emma Coxon,

for excellence in Reporting a Lecture on

"ALCOHOL AND THE HUMAN BODY."

Date *June 1 915.*

Annie Yorke

Office of the Union
59 & 60, Old Bailey, E.C.
CHARLES WAKELY, Sec.

President.

Societies promoting total abstinence from intoxicating drink among children first appeared around 1848. The United Kingdom Band of Hope Union was founded in 1855. Burton was a natural target for lecturers who spoke at chapel or church halls, often surrounded by brewery premises. Certificates were awarded to members who effectively reported to their own group afterwards on this ever-present threat to the youth of the town. (See page 96 for an extreme example of denunciation of drink).

One

Rediscovering the Past

Burton Snow Scene. St. Modwen's Orchard.
From "Burton Daily Mail" photo.

Stories from the distant past often take us back into the realms of legend. We are told how St Modwen, Burton's patron saint, performed many miracles, mostly as recorded in the writings of Geoffrey, sixth Abbot of Burton. One such account tells how a hermit named Hardulche from Bredon is visiting Modwen at 'the anchorage on Andressey' when a sudden storm capsizes a boat while 'two of her maidens' are crossing the Trent. Prayers for aid are answered by the waters of the Trent 'parting asunder' and allowing the holy pair to enter the river, find the sunken boat and save the 'maidens' from drowning. St Modwen's Orchard is the extremity of the Isle of Andressey, site of the original oratory of St Andrew, founded by Modwen. No traces of this or her later shrine have been found, but the spring called St Modwen's Well was once noted for its anti-scorbutic qualities (curing scurvy). The postcard has a timeless quality about it and conveys an impression of the 'waste land' chosen by St Modwen for her church.

Tatenhill cliff is probably the best known place locally for studying ancient geological strata. Until a hundred or so years ago there was an equally interesting view of a stratification on the opposite side of the Trent valley after the road was cut through up Bearwood Hill. The subsequent construction of the retaining walls, however, robbed this site of geological interest. The rare photograph shows the cliff face shortly before the walls were built.

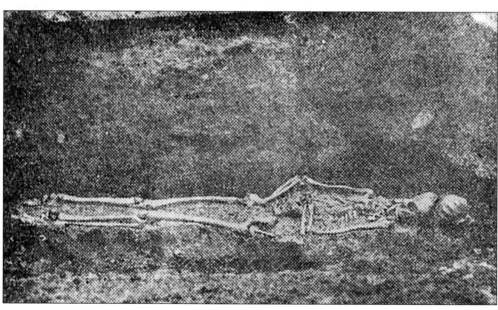

When it comes to 'meeting the ancestors' the earliest picture record has to be this 1881 photograph from excavations of an Anglo-Saxon cemetery and an earlier settlement site off Stanton Road, Stapenhill. Further excavations in 1953 established that there was a Romano-British native settlement occupied from the first to the fourth century AD. The area produced coins, pottery and metal work fragments, and quantities of animal bones associated with living sites of this period, typically situated on a hilltop, conveniently near to river and ford.

Repton became an important Anglo-Saxon centre and capital of Mercia until, in 874-5, Danish invaders in their longships came up this old course of the Trent, sacking Repton and wintering there before their conquest of Mercia. Archaeological investigations from the 1970s onwards by Professor Martin Biddle and Dr Taylor revealed much about those times. In this riverbank, above which extensive excavations took place, Professor Biddle found traces of a unique Viking dry-lock where boats could be hauled out of the river.

South Derbyshire acquired many spoil heaps and tips during its heyday of industrial activity. Most have disappeared–flattened or landscaped (plus the arrival of a ski slope). Few people passing Castle Gresley notice this feature (photographed around 1903 and locally called 'The Knob'), which has survived over 900 years. Imagine a surrounding ditch and stockade, stand on top, and you are where the new Norman lord of the manor lived in a wooden tower – Nigel de Stafford, ancestor of the Gresleys of Drakelow.

11

The engraving of Burton Abbey church in 1661 by Wenceslas Hollar is well known, though there are discrepancies with the accepted ground plan. Part became ruinous after the dissolution and in the Civil War stored gunpowder exploded causing further damage leading to final dismantling. This ruined interior of 1643, ascribed to Hollar, was subsequently revealed as a mid-nineteenth century forgery by John Thompson. It leaves us with no genuine interior view, but conveys a possible interpretation of the original grandeur.

In 1902, when new parish church vestries were being built, there was an opportunity for some small scale excavations. A trench in the market place revealed the line of foundations of the abbey church, dating back to the twelfth century, along the west front of the present building. The findings helped to confirm the accuracy of plans of the once great abbey of Burton founded by Wulfric Spot during the years 1002/04.

Save and other conservation groups are rightly concerned today about the condition of grade 2-listed Sinai Park. Recent individual attempts at partial restoration have produced some improvement and much of the fifteenth to seventeenth century interior has been mutilated, destroyed or exposed to the elements. This photograph depicts the reasonable condition 100 years ago when a farmhouse incorporated the original solar, chapel and cellar wing of this historic house, originally the sanatorium for the monks of Burton Abbey.

A striking photograph illustrating the work of medieval craftsmen in the roof of the building commonly known today as the Abbey. This building was originally the farmery or infirmary, standing away from the main abbey. The stout oak beams as viewed here may give an impression of haphazard arrangement but this is partly due to the angle at which the photograph was taken. They have certainly stood the test of time.

13

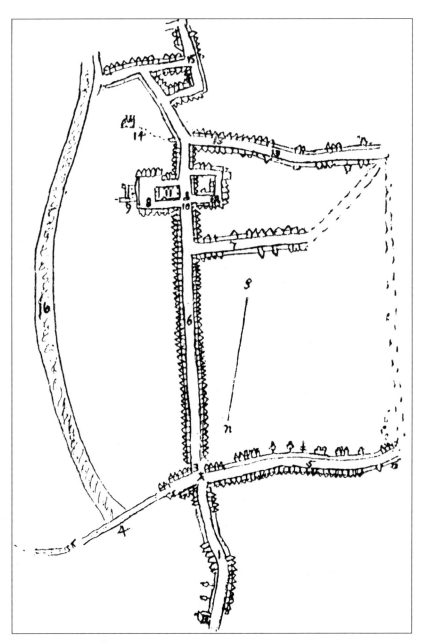

The oldest town map by Gregory King, dated 1679, shows how Burton grew parallel to the river with little development westwards. Horninglow Street ran over open common to Horninglow as did New Street to Shobnall. Cat (Catte) Street, later Station Street, was a mere stub but the open lane that became Guild Street is already defined. Note north side of Market Place named Church Street; and the scale using the old pole measure. A rod, pole or perch was $5\frac{1}{2}$ yards.

KEY to map. 1. Anderstaff Lane. 2. Mr Watson's Hall (not marked). 3. Mr Watson's Cross. 4. The bridge. 5. Horninglow Street. 6. High Street. 7. Cat Street. 8. Church Street. 9. The Church. 10. Market Cross. 11. Town Hall. 12. Swine Market. 13. New Street. 14. The Manor. 15. Lichfield Street. 16. River Trent.

MOORCROFT'S WHAREHOUSE.
CARRIERS BY FLY BOATS · COAL, COKE, SALT &.
103.

This photograph shows the remains of George Morecroft's Trent Navigation warehouse at the Soho, removed after the Ferry Bridge and viaduct opened in 1889. Horse-drawn fly boats carried coal, coke and Cheshire salt. Morecroft also operated steam mills on the Trent and Mersey canal at Barton Turns from 1838, manufacturing building cements, plaster of Paris, floor plaster, gypsum etc., and advertised supplies available at local inns, including the Bear and the Saracen's Head.

When the last properties formerly comprising the Soho were cleared in the 1960s for the development of Burton Technical College, an early eighteenth-century vault was unearthed under a row of cottages. It had been a store for casks of ale awaiting shipment down the Trent Navigation. Repaired and restored, it was incorporated into the centre for Students' Union activities.

Simnett's numbering of his earlier photographs is not always helpful for dating scenes but this view of Lichfield Street/New Street corner is Victorian, when Arthur Holmes's clothing emporium was one of the towns largest shops. By 1900 the corner site had become Boots the Chemist. A number of the properties here remain from Georgian times, at least as far as their upper storeys are concerned. Later rebuilding includes a new Dog Inn (Ye Dog in Georgian days). Well into the nineteenth century local maps showed Lichfield Street as Half Street, though this is an error concealing its true and fascinating historical source which was Haaf Street, a name belonging to times when Viking Danish invaders over-ran the district. It was a track that led to the river where the Danes could fish using their haaf nets (still used in some places today). Did Siward come down from Siwardsmoor (where Allsopps built a brewery)? The islands in the Trent still retain their old Danish names – Horseholm (Horsa's island) and Broadholme for example.

This scene perfectly illustrates the continuous threads that run through local history when rediscovering the past. Victorian Lichfield Street calls attention to surviving Georgian architecture. Take the name of the street 200 years ago and the clock turns back another 1,000 years to recall our Danish ancestors.

Actual accounts of daily life and public response in times before local newspapers are scarce, which makes all the more interesting a Burton editorial of 1860, recalling the 'village' of Georgian days and reflecting on changing attitudes.

'In the not very olden times when George IV was King (1820-30) Burton had many sources of instruction and amusement which it now possesses not. It had its theatre and its racecourse.

'The theatre was so conducted as to exact the approbation and patronage of nearly every inhabitant. The actors were talented artistes – some of great celebrity, who often enjoyed the personal friendship of the then élite of the town. The name of Miss Mellon, afterwards the good and charitable Duchess of St Albans, is still fresh in the reflections of many as an actress at the Burton Theatre.

'Burton races were celebrated in the annals of the turf and commanded the patronage and support of the noble and wealthy in the Midland district. In the days of which we are speaking Burton was, in comparison with its present wealth and importance, a mere village – but such a village!

'Neighbours met frequently then, courteous and social. Large parties met at jolly Christmas and on other festive occasions. Concerts, balls and card evenings were by no means infrequent and it was the fashion for everybody to speak well of and endeavour to do good to everybody. Would that those good old English times and customs existed now, but alas they do not. Certain 'French' notions began to spread abroad that this happy state of things was wrong. People discussed them; came to the conclusion that there was no harm in their amusements, but turned back on the way to theatre or race-course for the same reasons which many of them have for going to church, because on the whole it is perhaps more respectable! We are sorry to say that this is so, but our love of truth must compel us to admit that such is the humbug of the age in Burton – Burton the wealthy, the important, the great beer depot of the nation.

'Of a verity people who drink much beer, think beer. At length both theatre and racecourse became things of the past and both young and old regret that it is so. Now we defy all the bishops and parsons and curates in this land of ours to show that there is or can be anything but what is right and proper in all and everything that our Most Gracious Sovereign Lady the Queen does.'

Readers were reminded of Queen Victoria's appreciation of theatrical performances and of her regular visits to the Royal Ascot race meetings. (Her Majesty had not yet withdrawn from most public life, following the death of Prince Albert in 1861). 'We want some better recreations and amusements that we now possess. A good theatre would do much for us in the winter months. Re-establishing Burton races would afford a sort of annual carnival.'

Thus we have a brief impression of a small Georgian town losing its cosy 'village' character in trying to come to terms with changing times, the growth of industrialisation and the impact of the new ideas, development, growth and attitudes that heralded the Victorian era of rapid urban expansion.

NOTES: *The actual town population of Burton itself in 1821 was only 4,114. With the surrounding but still well separated districts of Stapenhill, Winshill, Branston, Horninglow and Stretton, the total was 7,043.*

The racecourse on Burton Meadow lasted from 1811 until 1840. (In the seventeenth and early eighteenth centuries there had been race meetings on the Outwoods). In our book Burton upon Trent – Tales of the Town, *see pages 12 and 13 for pictures and captions on the old Blue Posts (Burton's early theatre) and High Street Congregational Church, partly built with stone from the former race course grandstand.*

Until 1927 when Lichfield Street was widened the remains of the abbey gateway still stood facing New Street. Its position is marked by corners set into the roadway but a portion was re-erected in the private grounds of Newton Park, now a hotel, and with an old-type gas lamp preserved alongside. There is no public access to this feature.

Of actual abbey remains in situ a small portion of the cloister east wall and the parlour doorway have stood behind the market hall, neglected and lacking public access. C.H. Underhill in his 1941 History of Burton upon Trent, considered the condition of these relics to be a reproach to the town and that they should be better conserved. The position remained unchanged until an admirable recent decision to commemorate the Queen's Golden Jubilee by improving the abbey environs and facilitating public awareness and access.

The George Hotel in High Street probably enjoyed its hey-day in Georgian times when it was an important posting house for the Royal Mail coaches including the Standard and the Rapid. It became a popular family and commercial hotel until the late 1920s when the site was redeveloped. Though appropriate, its name was not attributable to the Georgian period; formerly it had been the George and Dragon inn.

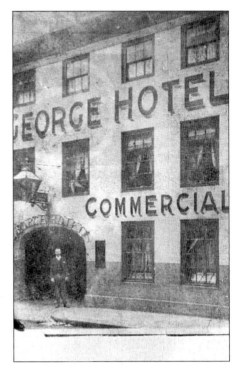

The family pose in front of another long lost Burton public house, the intriguingly named Foundry Inn. Selling Bindley's ales and adjoining their New Street brewery and malthouse, its name is a reminder that it stood opposite the iron foundry and engine works of Thornewill and Warham, who developed the site over nearly two centuries until 1929 when it was taken over by Briggs. Engineering has now given way to the Octagon shopping centre.

The eighteenth century White Horse was a typical small High Street inn already well established 200 years ago. Note that the National Provincial Bank (right) preceded its eventual demolition. It was replaced by the grandiose Market Hotel, which contrasted with the rather dour appearance of the White Horse, advertising its 'good stabling' and serving tea and coffee in its homely dining room.

Even Burton's surviving Victorian streets have tales to tell. There will already be many who don't recall the Market Hotel, although its upper façade remains. Cox and Malin's wine and spirits business later occupied the front portion. To the left was Richards, butcher; Parr's tiny bank (now a narrow shop); several small businesses; the Star Inn (once The Star of Bethlehem, later the Galaxy) and now unrecognisable as the old hostelry; Howarth's shoe shop and the original head Post Office. The small shops gave way to Woolworths before there was further redevelopment. If one thing remains unchanging in rediscovering the past, it is the continuous pattern of change.

Two
The Settlement of the Britons

3; Stanhope Bretby from The Spinney.

For over 1000 years Bretby has remained largely unspoilt with a succession of aristocratic landlords. It remained isolated as the Swadlincote area grew into an industrial conurbation, the Burton-Ashby road acting as a boundary between urban spread and undisturbed countryside. There is an old account illustrating the village's sense of community and the 'Britishness' of the men of Bretby from 750 years ago. The Sheriff of Derby was inquiring into the death of Robert, son of Henry de Bretteby. As had become judicial practice under Henry III, he 'took counsel of the neighbourhood.' On oath, 'good men' swore that his father killed Robert by misfortune and not by felony. Henry was ploughing in the field of Bretteby on Friday the morrow of St Mary Magdalene and his son, Robert, was driving the plough. Henry whirled the staff of the plough to frighten the oxen and horses. The iron of the staff being slightly fastened came off and struck Robert on the back of the head, so that he died of that wound, as the jury believes, on the Tuesday following. 'They say also that they know for a truth that Henry would rather have killed himself than his son because he had no other.'

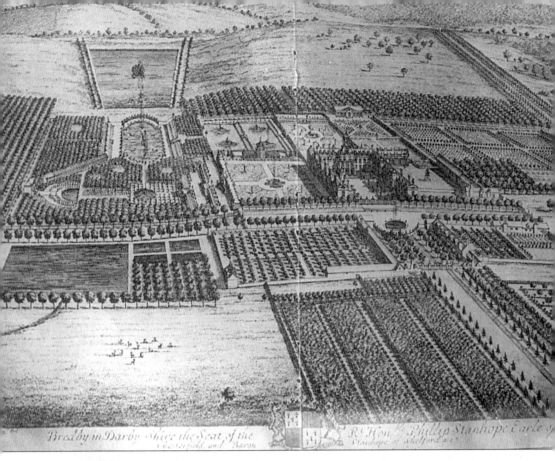

Bretby in Darby Shire the Seat of the Chesterfield and Baron   R.t Hon.le Phillip Stanhope Earle of Stanhope of Shelford &c.

Bretby first of all had its castle, foundations of which can be traced; then a succession of important houses, before becoming a place of great repute when the second Earl of Chesterfield rebuilt his mansion in the late seventeenth century and created a spectacular series of gardens. Designed by a Frenchman named Grillet, they were said to rival Versailles in France and were extensively visited by the aristocracy of the eighteenth century. Celia Fiennes, the intrepid early tourist, described visiting both house and gardens in 1698 and it was the latter that made Breby distinguished at this time. She especially admired three fountains containing elaborate water clocks, one with chimes that played Lilibolaro. The fifth Earl subsequently built the present hall and developed the parklands over the period 1780-1815. The notable gardens were abandoned but traces remain in the area called Philosopher's Wood – perhaps a potential site for future garden archaeology.

The later Earls were interested in developing their estates and in introducing good agricultural husbandry and dairying. The more pastoral aspect of the Bretby estate is seen in this Victorian engraving of the deer park. Early in the last century disposal of the property began and by 1915 the old family connections were ended, although the former Earls' family name of Stanhope is a reminder of their long association with Bretby, the name Stanhope Bretby being in common use.

Bretby passed to the Earls of Carnarvon in 1885, the fifth Earl, famed for his financing of the Tutankamen excavations in Egypt, disposing of the estate. Bretby Hall next opened as an orthopaedic hospital on 14 April 1926. Additional wards were built and the photograph recalls wards nine and ten in a block with facilities for patients to be moved outside. Hospital closure has introduced new phases in the Bretby story with the opening of a nursing home, conversions and developments of flats, including restoration of the hall, and new housing.

This unknown family had visits to the lakes and woods at Bretby recorded for their photograph albums. Invariably, even on a country outing, Edwardian visitors made few concessions as regards dress or formality but they are posed in settings which many people visited with great pleasure over the years. We have a wonderfully neat little hand-stitched school work book inscribed: 'Harriet Wright, Miss Challis's Seminary, Bretby Park, 24 June 1858.' In it Harriet did sums and texts in copperplate handwriting, entitling it 'Remembrances'. Seventy-six years later, in 1934, an elderly Harriet, obviously passing on her souvenir, shakily added on the cover: 'To show you how things were done in bygone days. In memory of many happy hours spent in Bretby Park.'

An intriguing picture, at first sight challenging one's observation, but in fact it represents a perfect study of natural camouflage. The photographer has recorded: 'Waterhen's nest, pond in Bretby Woods, 1911.' It is a reminder of the rich flora, fauna and bird life which still characterise this region and which were so closely observed and recorded by H.J. Wain, the Bretby naturalist and local historian.

The Bretby estate was acquired by Mr J.D. Wragg who had already leased the shooting rights from 1899. Previously the fifth Earl of Carnarvon had been a notable shot and distinguished shooting parties were a feature at the hall in the 1890s, a special train bringing them via Stanton to the halt at Stanhope Bretby. This picture shows pheasant rearing continuing at Bretby in the mid-1920s.

The cyclist, horseman and policeman are all intrigued by this Burton tram on Ashby Road near Bretby Lane. Although Burton Corporation laid and maintained track to the Borough boundary, they never ran a service on it, this being a test run for a braking system invented by P.J. Pringle, Burton tramways manager. He stands by the cab, where the driver is Inspector Peters. Burton and Ashby Light Railways trams operated through Stanhope Bretby to Swadlincote from 13 June 1906 and to Ashby from 2 July 1906.

The previous scene was an Edwardian postcard, sent from Bretby when Mrs Charity Ann Weddon was postmistress and this old cottage housed the village post office. Letters, via Burton, arrived at 6.45 a.m. and outgoing mail was dispatched at 6.50 p.m., Bretby then having its own postmark cancellation.

Brizlincote is an Anglo-Saxon name, and in 1850 it yielded up a fine sixth century brooch. The hall, described as 'Perhaps the finest small baroque house in England' is a 1714 rebuilding by the second Earl of Chesterfield. One tenant was William Nadin, whose sons, Joseph and Nathaniel, founded Nadin's colliery, but William's name designates the new road into Swadlincote. The hall became popular for outings (often by special trams) but here the resident family relaxes. The label suggests a tempting glass of Worthington White Shield.

GOLF HOUSE

For many, Bretby means golf. Burton Golf Club was established in 1894 off Woods Lane, Stapenhill, moving in 1897 to Branston. Wanting to enlarge from nine to eighteen holes, the club leased part of Oldicote Farm from the Earl of Carnarvon in 1907. The clubhouse design allowed conversion to a house if the venture failed. This might have happened in 1922 when a new course was considered opposite the Chesterfield Arms, but instead the freehold of the existing site was purchased. Today's clubhouse has expanded around the original, seen here in around 1914.

Above: Once popular makes of car appear in this 1920s advertisement for Parkes Garages at Swadlincote and Ashby. Many cars had canvas hoods, lowered for fine weather touring, while in some smaller models, junior passengers could be squeezed into a dickey seat which opened up to the rear of the two front seats (and you just had to hope it wouldn't rain!). There is also a roll call of many noted British motor cycles of those days. For some years Parkes operated Ashby-Burton buses after the tram service finished in 1927.

The twenties and thirties saw the start of mass motoring, and by 1939 there were nearly two million cars on the roads, more than twice as many as there were in 1929. Very significant had been the introduction of 'baby' cars such as the Austin 7 and the solid-tyred Trojan of 1922, with prices that fell from around £170 to little above £100 as Morris, Singer, Triumph, Clyno, Ford and others came on the scene. Petrol at two shillings (10p) a gallon in 1922 soon dropped to the equivalent of 5p or just over and was only 7/8p until 1938.

Opposite: First prize in Burton Shopping Week Draw, 1931, was a coach built Standard 4-door saloon worth £225. The winner was Mr Raymond Jones (twenty-four), whose mother ran a tobacconist's business at 51a Station Street. The winning ticket (C 21688) was one of 750,000 sold. With 610 prizes the draw lasted for 3½ hours. Mr Jones announced his intention of selling the car, obviously preferring to have the money. Money value in those days is indicated by a test monitored by the RAC in 1928 when a comparable car, a Rover 10 saloon, with four adults aboard, covered 2147 miles around England on one £5 note.

It is not generally realised that there was still an official (if largely ignored) 20mph speed limit in the 1920s but inevitably, in 1934, compulsory driving tests and 30mph speed limits were among new measures for road safety introduced by Leslie Hore-Belisha (still remembered for his crossings!).

GARAGE

Telephone 41
ASHBY-de-la-ZOUCH

...BY-DE-LA-ZOUCH

FOLLOWING CARS

...ANDARD ▪ SINGER

...y

16-35 h.p. £485

...TON, RALEIGH, TRIUMPH

...ween Ashby, Swadlincote and Burton

First Prize, **STANDARD COACH BUILT SALOON CAR**

OPEN DAILY

10 a.m. to 9 p.m.

SUNDAYS
INCLUDED

...THE...

GARDEN TEA ROOMS

(LOUNGE AND DINING ROOM),

ASHBY ROAD,
— BURTON. —

OPPOSITE BRETBY PARK, 5 MINUTES FROM CHESTERFIELD ARMS.

PARTIES
CATERED FOR
AT
Short Notice.

Around 1930 a recently built bungalow became the Garden Tea Rooms, no doubt encouraged by an increasing amount of tourist traffic on the Burton-Ashby road. Adjoining Bretby Park, more cars and motor cycles, plus the popularity of cycling (often in large groups), along with local walkers, suggested potentially good trade, especially at weekends. It proved to be a short-lived venture, but set out opening daily, including Sundays, which was quite rare at that time.

Three

A Pageant of Transport

The eighteenth century saw great developments in regard to local transport. In 1712 the Trent Navigation was opened to river transport and in 1770 the Burton section of the Trent and Mersey canal became operative. By 1780 the canal had largely superseded use of the Trent Navigation. During the second half of the century turnpike trusts began road improvements leading to great expansion of wagon and stagecoach provision. Canal and road services then suffered in turn when the Birmingham and Derby Railway opened through the town in 1837. Today's canal traffic is almost exclusively leisure-based and the big changes to the rail network have brought a return of people and goods to the country's over-crowded roads with all the associated problems of noise, congestion and pollution.

Horninglow basin on the Trent and Mersey canal thrived as a wharf and industrial site in the canal's earlier days, importing timber from the Baltic for the breweries and sending out beer supplies in return. This photograph by the late Ray Earp shows that there was still some commercial activity in 1970. In the background Ray has captured a memory of the once-familiar maroon and cream Burton Corporation buses.

One of few local coaching scenes, this 1837 painting by W. Clements shows 'Red Rover' operating a Liverpool-London service. It ran via the Dog and Partridge at Tutbury, the Three Queens at Burton, and via Ashby to Leicester. The side panels carried insignia of noted inns served by Robert Nelson's vehicles – the White Hart at Uttoxeter, the Three Queens, and the Three Cranes at Leicester. The painting visualises passengers enjoying fine weather but it could be a very different story!

Plan leaving Burton on the 9.15 a.m. train for Birmingham around 1899-1900. You live in Stapenhill, so can board Mr Wilkinson's horsebus by Stapenhill Green at 8.40 a.m. Via Trent Bridge, High Street and Station Street your journey to the station is scheduled for eighteen minutes. Catch the 5.45 p.m. return from Birmingham and you can comfortably board the 6.30 p.m. omnibus, due back in Stapenhill in just three minutes over the hour from your Birmingham departure. Has a century of progress improved on that?

Background for Repton's horse-drawn fire engine is almost certainly a street near Burton Town Hall, when it was taking part in one of the popular Edwardian processions. The photograph, with a Simnett series number, fits in with the 1909 Lifeboat Procession which included twelve engines from Burton Corporation, Bass's and Allsopp's breweries, Swadlincote, Uttoxeter, Tamworth, Lichfield and Repton – some long journeys for horse brigades; while one wonders about fire-fighting provision in their absence!

The shop of J. Jordan, clothier and draper (established 1885), was still at 25 Derby Street in the 1960s, suggesting a family succession. With this large horse-drawn wagon, from around 1900, Mr Jordan may possibly have had a country round supplying materials or delivering goods, a not uncommon practice. The thatched barn poses intriguing questions. Was it Mr Jordan's stable and situated near his business? From around 1887 touring theatrical companies sometimes performed at a 'wooden structure in Derby Street.' Could this conceivably have been their 'theatre', fitting their popular name of 'barnstormers?'

An act of 1903 enforced registration of motor vehicles, Burton being allocated the letters FA. This early dark blue 6hp (horse power) Benz has not yet received its number, FA 79. It was probably new when photographed outside the now demolished No. 62 Union Street on Duke Street corner, then the residence of surgeon Mr D.F.B. Cotes, seen with his chauffeur/mechanic in attendance. The General Infirmary was just down Duke Street, and over low buildings in between appears the 150ft spire of Christ church, dismantled as unsafe following the Fauld explosion of 1944.

Frank Reed (1880-1971), *Burton Mail* journalist and subsequently editor of the *Burton Observer*, on his $3\frac{1}{2}$ hp Triumph motor cycle (FA 210), photographed at Swadlincote, *c.* 1913. His wife, Lottie, is in the covered wickerwork sidecar. They sport traditional motor cycling headgear of the period – a large cap worn with the peak to the rear and, for the lady, a large bonnet tightly tied under the chin.

Until the 1960s much of the country's freight was carried by rail. Except for any coal wagons, it is likely that everything else conveyed by this typical mixed-goods train would now be road traffic. It is approaching Tutbury station from Derby (Nestle's chimneys in the background). The engine is North Staffs Railway 0-6-2 tank No. 77, but the absence of a company name suggests 1923 when the LMS came into being and No. 77 was to be renumbered 2239, lasting until 1927. Note the Moira colliery wagons in the siding.

Although a posed photograph, it certainly recalls memories of when elegant little brewery engines were a daily part of the local scene. Operating all over the town's extensive rail network, causing hold-ups at the innumerable level crossings, Bass engines (and those of other breweries) seemed a permanent feature. One could not imagine Burton without them but everything in this view has now gone. Note, however, how one cab-less engine in the centre did acquire a rather ungainly improvised cab.

Several breweries and other local firms used steam wagons for deliveries in the period prior to the Second World War. Marstons operated a regular run to Hampshire before switching to lorries. One of the last firms using Sentinel steam wagons was Everards of Leicester who had a brewery in Burton from 1886 (Meadow Road), moving in 1898 to Anglesey Road (closed in 1985). This vehicle is parked outside the former Guild Street school, which later housed the School of Speech and Drama and the Little Theatre.

For King George V's Coronation on 22 June, 1911, Burton's trams were decorated and used as grandstands (charge, three pence per head) to view the town's celebration procession. Prizes were awarded for the two best decorated covered cars and the two best open-top cars. Motormen, wives and helpers prepared the trams overnight. Here they are lined up in Horninglow Street, with a winning car at the front. One tram was painted white with a Maltese Cross to act as a first-aid ambulance, manned by the St John Ambulance Association.

In our earlier volume on East Staffordshire we included an interior scene of Leafield Farm on School Green at Yoxall. This fine study of a horseman actually appears as a framed picture in another interior scene. It typifies the Edwardian country gentlemen or farmer, for whom horseback would be the customary means of solo travel around the district.

From a local album comes this reminder of the great popularity of cycling in Edwardian times when a range of machines, usually costing between £5 and £10 new, perhaps £2 second hand, offered 'healthy exercise and personal transport' for men, women and children. This is a neat study of a lady's bicycle and its rider, full of detail as regards both machine and costume.

BASS & Co.'s
EXCURSION.
FRIDAY, JUNE 25th, 1875.

To LONDON (St. Pancras Station) **& the CRYSTAL PALACE.**

The following arrangements must be observed by Persons going by the
LONDON TRAIN:

BASS & Co.'s No. 4 TRAIN, FOR LONDON ONLY, (St. Pancras Station,)
will leave the BURTON MIDLAND TIMBER WHARF, (adjoining Bass & Co.'s Mosley Street premises,) precisely
at 4·30 a.m., calling at ASHBY at 4·50 a.m., and arriving at St. Pancras Station about 9·5 a.m.

The Return Train will leave St. PANCRAS STATION precisely at 9·15 p.m., calling at BEDFORD and
ASHBY as in going, arriving at Burton about 1·35 a.m. (Saturday.)

Persons holding these Excursion Tickets, and who may have received permission from the Head of their Department to prolong their stay in London, will be allowed to return from St. PANCRAS STATION, BY ANY TRAIN,
upon any day up to and including THURSDAY, JULY 1st, upon payment of 2s. each at the BOOKING
OFFICE, St. PANCRAS STATION.

Passengers may alight at BEDFORD for 10 minutes both going and returning, but they are particularly
requested to resume their seats in due time, on both occasions, so that the Train may not be delayed, BEDFORD
being the only authorised place of stopping, where passengers may alight, they are strongly cautioned against leaving
their seats in the Train at any other point.

Persons are requested to be at the Station at least 10 minutes before the time fixed for the departure of the Train
from Burton & St. Pancras.

It is particularly requested that the men will not leave the Carriages while the train is in motion, and only enter
the class of carriage for which they have tickets; they are also requested to be quiet and orderly, not to damage the
carriages in any way, and to assist their Foremen in carrying out the before-named regulations.

INSURANCE TICKETS can be obtained at the time the excursion tickets are given out, on application to
MR. W. WALTERS.

Should any of the men have any enquiry or complaint to make they are requested to see the Head of their
Department.

☞ Upon the arrival of the Train at St. Pancras, a TELEGRAM will be sent to Burton announcing the same,
which will be exhibited on the Old Brewery Yard Doors, in High Street; a similar Telegram will also be
sent to Mr. HAWKINS, at the Midland Railway Station, Burton. The information contained in these
messages will be for the friends of the Excursionists, and may be relied upon as being true.

Edwardian Bass trips are well recorded, but earlier excursions much less so and with as little pictorial record. They began in 1865 when two trains went to Liverpool. After a river trip there was a dinner with long speeches, leaving little time before returning home. In 1867 two trains went to the Crystal Palace at Sydenham, with gratuities in lieu of the dinner. Trips remained biennial until 1883, when they became an annual event. This is part of the 1875 notice of three trains for the Crystal Palace again, a fourth for 'London only'.

Here are all the makings of convivial all-male works picnic in which a pint of ale plays a central role! Details are unfortunately lacking other than that it is a Burton gas works trip in the 1920s. It looks as though squeezing all thirty aboard could be a tight fit. The driver's cap badge confirms that this is a Trent motor bus.

Four
Lost Gardens

Molyneux, the local historian (1869) refers to Stapenhill Hall (sic) as a 'fine brick building of the seventeenth century'. The house remained until the 1930s when Burton Corporation acquired the site to develop Stapenhill Gardens. Prior to its demolition Stapenhill House grounds were well concealed behind high brick walls and only recently have we found photographs revealing the original gardens. The house itself comprised a full range of handsome ground floor rooms, ten principal bedrooms and eleven other bedrooms in the attic area. A bathroom, lavatory and W.C. are listed in a sale notice of 1911. Stables, coach/motor house, various outbuildings and an extensive range of greenhouses were among the outdoor features. In its final years Stapenhill House was the residence of the Goodgers, Burton solicitors, who subsequently moved to Andersley House in Spring Terrace Road.

Stapenhill House backed on to Main Street so most views show the front aspect with a garden of lawns, flower beds and shrubberies approached from the house through an ornamental porch.

This view from the porch towards the steps descending to a lower garden is broadly recognisable today. Many trees have been cleared but a pair of beech trees still frame a view across the river towards the town. Earlier this was evidently not appreciated, with regard to the heavy growth of foliage along the riverbank below. After descending a further long flight of stone steps, one looked back up to the house. Either side, logs supported grass terracing, lined with rather heavy and solid hedging. Where the ornamental swan is situated today was laid out as a tennis court and, at about the point where St Peter's Bridge now crosses, there was the family boat-house.

The most prolific part of the garden was based on the sunny slopes adjoining Jerrams Lane, this splendid scene showing it all to advantage. The extensive area under glass included a conservatory, vinery, peach house and orchard house as well as the conventional greenhouses. The kitchen garden included a wide range of small fruit bushes and mature fruit trees.

Councillor Mrs Mary Goodger J.P. of Stapenhill House, who served as Burton's first Lady Mayor for the year 1931/32. This portrait shows her in ceremonial robes and offers a good close-up of the Mayoral chain of office.

The Round Garden, Drakelowe

At the same time as the original Stapenhill House gardens were being re-established, the notable gardens of Drakelow Hall (demolished 1934) were lost. Not normally viewed by the public, paintings of the garden were, however, commissioned for use on coloured picture postcards. The attractive Round Garden was featured in an Edwardian series *Gardens of England*; the rose garden was painted in 1925, both scenes by the same artist, Beatrice Parsons. At one time an outdoor staff of thirty had tended the various enclosed gardens at Drakelow. After the power station was established, a replica of the Round Garden fountain was installed as a decorative feature adjoining the power station canteen.

Standing above road level few people will have looked into the main garden of Bearwood House (former home of the Gothards) situated across the road from their residence. Construction of new housing means that another delightful garden has disappeared under bricks and mortar. This is a scene from around 1905, and shows much of the original garden (roofs on the right were then newly built houses in Osborne Street). Of additional interest is a pony drawing the mower and wearing canvas 'boots' to protect the lawn.

HOLLAND HOUSE
BARTON UNDER NEEDWOOD.

The Holland family was associated with Barton under Needwood for over 600 years until the 1950s. Holland House with its garden (typical mid-Victorian) was then demolished. This house was often let out to tenants, family members residing in other village properties. It stood off Station Road and the site is now Meadow Rise. The family name is recalled by Holland Park estate, opposite, and by the Holland Sports Club, on land donated by the family.

Henry Tooth established Bretby Art Pottery in 1883 and also built two big houses on Burton Road, Woodville. One was Tresco (centre) which survives; the other was his own residence, Hazeldene (left). A large lawn behind those two houses was often used for staging charity events. Popular in Edwardian days was a Pageant of Living Whist and this scene shows 'The Shuffle' in progress. Hazeldene has been demolished and a nursing home now occupies the performance area.

Although not a private garden, this is a revealing study of the Cherry Orchard, Burton, as it appeared as late as the 1930s. Immaculately maintained from Victorian times as a small public amenity with a resident steward on site in a neat little cottage, it is a reminder of days when vandalism, graffiti, litter and despoiling of public places were not tolerated.

Five
Working at Caldwell Hall

Many big houses in the area, once private residences, have been demolished or adapted for other purposes. They once provided considerable opportunities for local employment but it was a way of life that remains today only as a memory.

In 1934 Jessie May Tooth, born at Hartshorne, went into service at Caldwell Hall, home of the Milligans, as third housemaid. She thus began near the bottom of the 'downstairs' hierarchy, a pattern of social order which still pertained in the servants' quarters of large houses. Of an indoor staff of twelve, the housekeeper, cook, butler and two ladies' maids were in a group above that of footman, three housemaids, kitchen maid and scullery maid, each group having its own separate room for meals. When Jessie began work there was also a hall boy. In addition, there was an outside staff of about six gardeners, groom, a chauffeur and farm bailiff.

Caldwell ('the cold spring or stream') has a long history, the manor being given to Burton Abbey by William the Conqueror. Three ancient little windows in the much-restored church are last remnants of possible pre-Norman establishment. Part of the hall dates back to 1678 but it is mainly Georgian. Caldwell was sold in 1858 to Sir Henry des Voeux, who donated the clock for Swadlincote market hall; it then passed in 1875 to his nephew, Colonel Charles Milligan.

This family comprised eight members, listed here in assorted order, to show the curiosity of an alphabetical list of names.

Ada (daughter) died 1951 aged 85
Blanche (daughter) died 1953 aged 78
Charles (Colonel Milligan) died 1902
Dunbar (George) died aged 45
Eva (daughter) died 1960 aged 98 (last of the line)
Frank (son) died 1900 aged 30 (Boer War)
Gertrude (the Colonel's wife)
Hilda (daughter) died aged 40.

Perhaps George was always known as Dunbar to preserve this sequence. There are often references to the Colonel's three daughters but there was a fourth, Hilda, who was little known and seldom seen. When Jessie Tooth arrived at Caldwell it was indeed the home of 'the three

Miss Milligans'. Eva Gertrude as the eldest was, of course, always titled Miss Milligan. Jessie remembers her as a demure, serene, very 'ladylike' person. Ada Catherine was a religious woman and an invalid, the staff subsequently including two nurses to care for her. Blanche Justina was the dominant figure – eccentric and very much 'the boss' – in fact, the staff regarded her as a 'right Tartar'.

The housemaids began work at 6 a.m. and remained on duty until the ladies had retired. A last task was to fill hot water bottles, the only time housemaids were allowed to enter the kitchen. Duty began with clearing, cleaning and black-leading grates and lighting fires required that day. Rooms were all elaborately furnished and overcrowded with ornaments, all of which had to be kept dusted or polished. The maids made their own beeswax polish and also made up a mixture of vinegar and salt used for cleaning copper pans.

Another task was filling hip baths, which were used throughout the house as there was only one bathroom, for Miss Milligan's use. A second bathroom was added on the top floor shortly before the war. Coal and coke fired stoves and ranges heated water and were used for all the cooking. Electric lighting was installed but there were few household gadgets or domestic aids to relieve the brush and dustpan routine, except once a year when Messrs Ordish and Hall of Burton performed an annual spring clean, bringing their own staff and equipment.

In contrast to the main rooms the servants' accommodation was meagre, although Jessie's bedroom was south facing on the top floor overlooking the garden: 'Unfortunately there was never time to go up there and enjoy the view'. The housemaids had one half day a week and an alternate Sunday half-day after completion of duties, and provided that they had attended church first. This involved a walk to Rosliston for a morning service or Caldwell for early evening. A bicycle was needed for most outings, as there was only an occasional Burton bus from Rosliston, while for Swadlincote one had to get to Gresley first.

Meal times were announced by the ringing of the bell on the roof over the stable clock. The ladies – 'Blanche in charge' – did some shopping by car, but regular bulk supplies came from the Army and Navy Stores in London. The servants' basic supplies were rationed out, even before the war, so that, for example, everyone had their own butter dish and a supply to last the week. It was the Second World War that took Jessie away from the hall.

Miss Blanche was a leading organizer for the Women's Land Army, and wanted to retain Jessie for a local unit (and no doubt other duties as well!), so Jessie made the break in 1941 and served with the NAAFI. She did not return to Caldwell, and the old order at the hall was soon to change as the three ladies, who had spent all their lives there, ended their days – Ada in 1951, Blanche in 1953 and then Eva in 1960, to bring to an end the story of the Miss Milligans of Caldwell. Another country house was sold and its contents auctioned and scattered. The house survives as a special school and as the witness to a very different life style.

Opposite: The Army and Navy Stores, established in 1871, supplied every imaginable item from provisions to motor cars and from footwear to full-size billiard tables, for use at home or overseas, especially for the British in India. They published an annual hard-back catalogue of over 1,100 pages, and were an obvious choice for bulk supplies by a military gentlemen like Colonel Milligan, the family continuing the routine. The catalogue extract includes items Jessie remembers being regularly supplied in quantity to Caldwell. Not included on the page is the beeswax, which came in large blocks, or the hard yellow scrubbing soap supplied in long bars, which the maids had to wipe dry every time after use to help conserve them. The page reproduced does include various polishes and cleaners including 'Town Talk' silver polish, tins of Harpic ('reaches right round the bend'), and different kinds of dusters and cloths which came in dozens.

POLISHING CLOTHS, DUSTERS AND POLISHES.

[RE]DIO" IMPREGNATED [P]OLISHING CLOTHS.

No Liquids or Paste required.

Brass and Copper .. .. −/7½
Silver, Gold and Plate .. −/7½
[fo]r Nickel, Aluminium, Chromium
[Pla]ter .. .. .. −/7½
[Dou]ble Size for any of the above,
each 1/2
.. .. −/7½
[Finishing] Cloths, for use after above,
Yellow. each −/4½; doz. 4/−

THE "POLI" CLOTHS.
T.G. 274.

Unrivalled for polishing Glass, Silver, Furniture, Motor-cars, Leather, etc.
Size, 27 × 27 in. .. −/9
" 22 × 22 " .. −/7

POLISHING CLOTHS.
T.G. 275.

Stockinette .. −/2½, −/4½
Approx. size 20 × 18 in.
Yellow .. −/4½; doz. 4/−
Approx. size 25 × 24 in.
Chamois −/8; doz. 7/6

CHECK DUSTERS.
T.G. 276.

[Si]ze 24 × 22 in., .. −/5 ; doz. 4/9
[Si]ze 26 × 24 in. .. −/7½; doz. 7/3

[NUB]BIE" DUSTLESS DUSTER.
T.G. 277.

[Specially] prepared Cloth. Each 1/−

[ST]OCKINETTE CLOTH.
T.G. 278.

[f]or Motor or Household use.
50 yards .. per roll 4/−
25 " .. " " 2/3

SPONGE CLOTHS.
T.G. 279.

[cleani]ng purposes, size 24 × 24 in.,
each −/3, doz. 2/6

[S]COURING CLOTHS, DUSTERS, Etc.
T.G. 280.

[Cl]oths .. per lb. −/11; per 28 lb. 24/6
Flannel .. per yard −/10
" per roll of 45 yds. 36/−
" Best quality per yard 1/9
" per roll 50 yards 80/−
[f]or Paint Cloths .. each −/5, −/7
doz. 4/6, 6/6

COTTON WASTE.
T.G. 281.

[Wa]ste .. .. per cwt. 59/−
7   14   28   56 lb
3/9   7/6   15/−   30/−
[Whit]e Waste .. .. per cwt. 69/6
5/−   9/9   19/6   38/−
including weight of bag, sent direct
[fro]m Makers, carriage not paid.

T.G. 282.
Just sprinkle at night and flush next morning
—the work is done.
Tin .. .. −/6, 1/−, 1/9

"DOBY" CLEANSER.
T.G. 283.

Cleans anything and everything. Will not affect the hands. Will remove rust, dirt, cleans paintwork, lino, carpets, rugs, etc.

½ pt. 1 pt. 1 qt. gal.
Per tin −/6, 1/−, 1/9, 6/−*

*To order.

LIQUID VENEER.
T.G. 284.

A good renovator for all classes of furniture, etc.
Price per bottle .. .. 1/6, 3/−, 6/−

"TOWN TALK" SILVER POLISH
T.G. 285.

Per bottle, −/8, 1/4, 2/6

"TOWN TALK" SILVER PLATE CLOTHS.
T.G. 286.

In packets 1/6

"TOWN TALK" CHROMIUM PLATE CLOTHS.
T.G. 287.

1/6 each.

"ROZALEX."
(British Made.)

T.G. 288. It is non-greasy, non-caustic. Keeps the hands free from chaps and cracks. Prevents dirt and grease coming in contact with the skin.
Per tube .. .. 1/−
Per tin 2/6

HOUSEHOLD LUBRICANT.
T.G. 289.

A most useful Oil for the house ; for Sewing Machines, Typewriters, Lawn Mowers, Hand Separators, Guns, etc.
Tin .. .. −/6

"RONUK" FLOOR POLISH.
T.G. 290.

For cleaning and polishing Parquet, Stained Wood, Linoleum, etc.

Per tin −/10, 1/6, 2/6
5 lb., 8/−; 10 lb., 12/6

"RONUK" FLOOR DRESSING
T.G. 291.

For renovating and polishing Wood Bl[ocks]
Parquet, and Stained Floors, Linoleum,
1 pt., 2/−; 1 qt., 4/−; 1 gal., 15/−

HOSPITAL "RONUK" CONCENTRATED.
T.G. 292.

7 lb. tins .. .. .. each [..]
14 " " .. .. " 1[..]

MAPLE LIQUID FLOOR AND FURNITURE POLISH
T.G. 293.

Cleans and polishes in one operation. In
1/−, 1/9, 3/−, and 7/− (½ gall.)

THE "QUIXIE" HOUSEHOLD WAX POLISH.
T.G. 294.

For cleaning and polishing Linoleum, Fl[oors]
of every description, Paint, Marble Leat[her]
and Motor Cars.
Per tin .. .. 1/−,
Per 3 lb. tin .. .. .. [..]

JACKSON'S CAMPHORATED WAX POLIS[H]
T.G. 295.

For Stained Floors, etc., 1/−
1 lb. tins, 1/9 ; 2 lb., 3/− ; 4 lb., [..]
*7 lb., 10/−

*To order.

JACKSON'S LAVENDER FURNITURE CREA[M]
T.G. 296.

In Doulton Art Jars. For Valuable Poli[sh]
Woodwork of all kinds, −/10, 1/6 and [..]

"JOHNSON'S" BALLROOM FLOOR WAX.
T.G. 297.

For Dancing Floors. Sprinkle lightly over [the]
floor, and the feet of the dancers will do the [rest]
Per tin 2/6

"JOHNSON'S WAX."
T.G. 298.

Johnson's Prepared Wax brings out [the]
patterns of lino and floor cloths, pol[ishes]
Floors, Piano, Furniture, etc.. etc.
Per tin .. .. −/10½, 1/6
Liquid Wax, for Furniture per b[ottle]
1/−, 2/6

JOHNSON'S GLOCOAT.
T.G. 299.

The new Floor Polish. Needs no rub[bing.]
Apply with Duster.
½ pt., 1/6 ; 1 pt., 2/9 ; 1 qt., 5/−

THE "O-CEDAR" WAX POL[ISH]
T.G. 300

Unrivalled for floors and linoleum,
Per tin −/10, 1/7½, 3/−. 4 lbs. 5/9. 7 lbs[.]

O-CEDAR WAX CREAM.
T.G. 301.

Provides a new and astonishingly easy [and]
efficient method of combined cleaning [and]
polishing. Polishes almost everything [in]
the home. Sold in glass containers.
Sizes −/9, 1/6.

RENTOKIL FURNITURE CRE[AM]
T.G. 302.

Cleans, polishes, preserves and pre[vents]
attacks on furniture by Worm, Beetle, or [..]
Price, 4 oz. 1/−; 8 oz. 1/9; 12 oz. [..]

ALL PRICES ARE SUBJECT TO MARKET FLUCTUATIONS.

The south front of Caldwell Hall, overlooking the park. The view could be enjoyed, from left to right: the bow-windowed drawing room; the library; the study and the dining room. Principle bathrooms were on the first floor where Miss Ada and Miss Eva had their rooms. The attics were sparse accommodation for the servants and Jessie Tooth's room had the middle window on the attic floor. In this scene from the early 1900s, tennis and croquet are set out on the front lawn. Miss Blanche's room was in a wing on the north entrance front where she could view visitors and keep a close eye on the domestic staff. Over the rear stable block was a turret containing an ancient bell inscribed 'Cast by Battrene, Graysley 1578'. It was rung for meal times and had been mended in 1896 by Joseph Wood, the Caldwell blacksmith, after being declared beyond repair.

The small agricultural village of 'Cauldwell' (alternative spelling) had a population of under 200 but even the rare appearance of a photographer doesn't seem to have caused any interest.

Six
Commercial Gentlemen

Another way of life changed after the First World War with the development of cheap but reliable small motor cars – that of the commercial traveller, previously catered for by the railway companies. Often he might leave his hometown on a Monday with a quantity of stock and samples and set himself up for the week at a convenient hotel, visiting all his local customers before returning home at the weekend. The Midland Railway allowed commercial travellers (along with other special groups like theatrical performers) to carry up to 3cwt (hundredweight) of luggage with a first class ticket (or 1½cwt third class). Porters would meet the trains, install the owner and his baggage in a conveyance, and he would then make his way to his hotel ready for visits around the district. Let us follow a commercial gentlemen to the Queens' Hotel, Burton, his base for a week's work locally.

A 'just arrived' postcard could be purchased at railway bookstalls, quickly filled in and posted in the station letterbox. The character pictured here seems to fancy a relaxing visit but as the sender reports that he is based at the Station Hotel, it is likely that he too is a commercial traveller advising his arrival in Burton.

Reaching the Queens' Hotel our traveller would have found Bridge Street a busier and more important shopping area than was later the case. Traffic-wise, however, it was quiet enough for two young ladies to chat in the middle of the tramlines. Note that the Queens' was not yet a corner site, Wetmore Road being narrow with quite a substantial shop adjoining the hotel. It was demolished in the 1920s when the Corporation opened up Wetmore bus park.

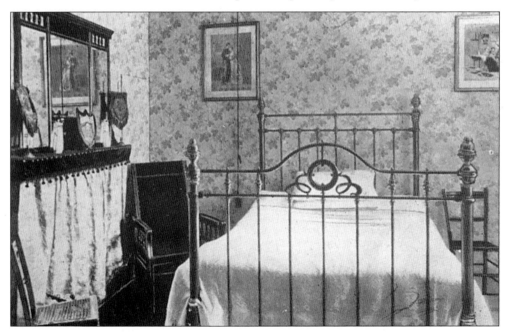

A single bedroom would cost 3 shillings (15p) per day. Probably with clerical work and book-keeping to be dealt with the traveller would engage a private sitting room where he could also relax from his labours, and this would cost $12\frac{1}{2}$p per day. Additional extras might include a fire in his bedroom (5p per day) and arrangements for a welcome hot bath for $2\frac{1}{2}$p.

The sitting room no doubt reminded many visitors of their own front parlour at home – rather overcrowded, the walls covered with pictures. Note two very typical features of the period – the aspidistra plant and the day-bed sofa for the strongly recommended after lunch rest.

Our man probably joined fellow travellers for his meals in the Commercial Room where breakfast and luncheon were served from 10p per head, with a plain tea if required at a charge of 5p. Dinner at the end of the day's work would offer a wide-ranging menu with charges from 15p. In the provinces it was still usual for meals to be served at one large table. The late Victorian introduction of separate tables in London hotels had not yet become general practice.

Afterwards one might adjourn to a formal coffee room, or perhaps, more informally, meet up with acquaintances in the Smoke Room where ales were supplied by Marston's. Many commercial gentlemen followed this pattern of life, going home for the weekend before setting out again with order book and samples to cover the next area on their itinerary.

Interestingly, the 1900 Burton trades directory listed thirty-seven commercial travellers residing in the town. From their individual addresses it has been possible to divide them up into eighteen brewer's travellers, one grocer's, one tailor's and one timber merchant's traveller; plus sixteen listed simply as 'traveller' or 'commercial traveller'.

Seven
The Day's Work

These pictures from around the district reflect on a range of local occupations and illustrate the ever-changing shape of the local industrial scene and of employment patterns in the everyday life of town and country.

Three Burton firms once manufactured motor cars locally – Salmon, Baguley and the Ryknield Engine Co. Ltd, who operated from 1902 until 1910 on Shobnall Road. Ryknield cars, commercial vehicles and buses were individually assembled and here we have smartly attired employees of the erecting department in a photograph precisely dated 18 April 1907. A large chassis stands over a pit ready to receive its frame. Note the solid rubber tyres and the large cooling fan. The company's top range cars were priced up to £700, comparable with a Rolls Royce of the period.

Relaxation time for employees of C.S. Spooner, of the noted partnership of Orton and Spooner, makers of all types of fairground equipment. Obviously a light-hearted occasion, even if they all look very solemn posing in a roundabout motor car (wheels on one side only) awaiting adornment in Spooner's workshop. Quantities of timber can be seen which will become fairground features, carved in great detail and subsequently gilded in many exotic colours to grace the popular travelling fairs of the day.

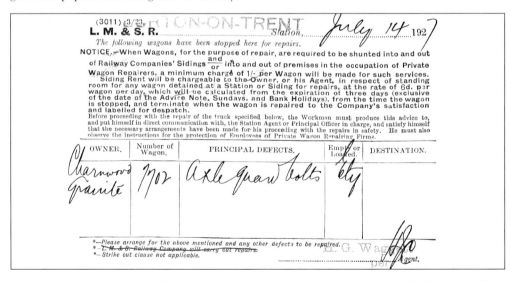

A reminder of the innumerable tasks undertaken by railway employees in the hey-day of rail transport. Apart from coal and mineral wagons there were, in 1925, 700,000 private owner wagons, many of special design for particular cargoes. Besides collecting and returning them they needed examining for faults that might jeopardise safety. Here Mr Waggett, the goods agent, notifies Charnwood Granite Quarries that they must rectify a defect on one of their wagons held back at Burton in 1927.

100 years ago there were twenty-two shoeing and general smiths in Burton, while every village had at least one blacksmith who, apart from working with the horse population, could generally turn his hand to any local job. Bass brewery had their own blacksmiths' shop on a grand scale – fifteen forges, 8cwt steam hammer, machines for drilling, screwing, punching and shearing, and two shoeing shops. As the photograph shows, many smiths were employed in one of the town's noisiest workshops. The joiners' shop survives, converted into the Bass Museum.

Views of work in progress on a brewery malting floor are scarce, but this photograph, from around 1911, shows barley being turned at Ind Coope's maltings. A 'piece walker' was responsible for each 'piece' or area of barley, his gang of six regulating the temperature of the germinating barley by raking, ploughing with a plough stick (right centre) or turning with malt shovels. On reaching the required germination stage the barley was transferred to a roasting kiln to be cured and dried, and was then known as malt.

Burton Corporation Fire Brigade moved from Union Street to fine new headquarters in New Street (now a garage) in 1903. There were also brigades at Bass's and Allsopp's breweries, and hose reel stations at the foot of Bearwood Hill; the Barley Mow, Stapenhill; near the Mission Room in Horninglow; the Market Hall; in Byrkley Street; and at Broadway school. This photograph is probably just post World War One. Mr R.W. Gooch was the long-serving Superintendent and he was succeeded by his son, W. Gooch (middle-row, fourth from the left). On the back row, second from the left is Norman Hird, stoker on the steam fire engine which, like the horse ambulance, was shortly to be replaced by motor vehicles. Memorable local fires early in the century included Perk's timber yard in Lichfield Street, Peach's maltings in Wood Street and Eadie's spirit stores in Cross Street. J.S. Simnett, the photographer, was among the part-time firemen who would leave their work and rush to the station as quickly as possible on receiving a call. The full-time firemen mostly lived conveniently near, in Union Street and New Street.

T.G. Green established a pottery at Gresley in 1790 that still thrives today. In July 1904 the factory suffered a serious fire which put many employees out of work. The extent of the damage is clear from this photograph, which shows only some of the destruction. Swadlincote and Burton fire brigades fought the blaze though with horse-drawn engines; the latter faced a long and tough journey out. Catastrophes of this sort could rob a man of his day's work leaving him without income, often with sad consequences for his family.

Casks and crates being loaded for delivery by lorries of Ind Coope's fleet in the early 1920s. This area now houses the Imex Business Park and the view looks back towards Moor Street bridge and the main line (with a passenger train approaching the station). The Railway Mission Hall shows up on the left with Burton South signal box to the right. Note the women employees, who probably began work during labour shortages in World War One, altering the whole traditional employment pattern.

It is July 1907 and 'everyone is busy on the hay and Auntie has to be up on the rick'. Other farm activities have to go on as usual, however, and in this scene from Rolleston it is milking time. It is taking place in an open cowshed under conditions that were perfectly normal and acceptable at that period. Note the traditional milking stools. The writer proudly adds: 'What do you think of our cows?'

This traditional haymaking scene was photographed in South Derbyshire and it illustrates the message accompanying the previous picture, 'everyone is busy on the hay'. We have a youngster leading the horse and a woman in long black skirt helping to load. Once cut, the hope was for fine weather so that the hay could be turned and gathered in quickly. The cut swathes show up clearly and had to be raked up for loading.

Few streets within the grid layout of workers' town houses were far from a chip sho – always listed as 'fish fryers'. Picture records seemed unlikely – not surprising, as they would hardly attract photographers. One 1920s scene has come to light, however, the saloon of Mrs R. Mullis at No. 20 Horninglow Street (near Guild Street junction). This lady, we learn, was determined to establish her own business and both achieved her aim and had herself photographed proudly posing in the doorway. No. 20 and adjoining properties have all since gone.

Who makes good Kettles and strong Cans,
Good Porridge Saucepans and Ash Pans,
Good Dripping Tins and Toilet Cans?

Will Grimsley!

Who makes strong Colanders for peas,
And makes good Urns for children's teas?
And if you order one, you'll please

Will Grimsley.

Who makes Stove Pipes and Backdraughts too,
And understands his trade right through,
And makes Washups that will please you?

Will Grimsley!

Tell me the man who's in the trade,
Who at German Toys is not afraid,
And keeps Toy Engines, Stapenhill made?

Will Grimsley!

In Victorian times there were many skilled tradesmen around the town who produced hand-made everyday items. Will Grimsley of No. 40 Woods Lane, Stapenhill, was described as a 'wholesale and retail iron, tin and zinc worker'. In the programme for the 1897 Jubilee Fair at Stapenhill Institute, his advertisement comprised original verses listing some of the many different things he could make in his own workshop to supply local needs combining quality with cheapness.

A still-recalled Burton memory is of the level crossings, which thwarted traffic and pedestrians alike. Meet a man who rang his bell and then closed the crossing gates just before you could manage to dash across. This is Wilfred Birkin, signalman at Bass's Station Street gate box in the late 1950s. From Middle Brewery his view looked across Station Street to the New Brewery and Delhi maltings, all now swept away. The wheel controlling the gates is just in view, left.

Eight
A High Street Mystery

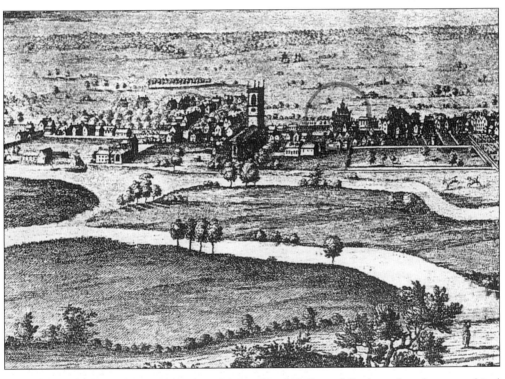

In the first half of the eighteenth century, Samuel and Nathaniel Buck produced topographical engravings from all around the country. We are indebted to them because they provided 515 scenes, a wonderful pictorial record of the period. 428 were views of abbeys, castles, etc., four were country seats; and eighty-three were general views of towns, including Burton upon Trent visited in 1732.

Most people are familiar with Buck's East Prospect of Burton, which has often been reproduced (only a small section is shown above). There is, however, one feature on it (ringed) which might have been expected to stimulate inquiry but which seems to have aroused little interest, although it 'sticks out like a sore thumb'. Rising well above the roof-lines of the rest of the town is an ornate, highly decorative building. What was it? Where was it situated? How is it that such a prominent structure has received scant attention? Even local historians of the past have little to say date-wise and have only generalised about its history.

In coaching days there were three posting inns for coaches and wagons communicating with Derby, Nottingham, Sheffield, Manchester and Birmingham. They were the Three Queens, the George and the Crown. Molyneux (published 1869) mentioning the Crown Inn says: 'This well-known inn formed part of the house and premises now occupied by Mr Birch. In an old view of Burton either this or an adjoining house is shown as of considerable height and curiously decorated'. This has to refer to Buck's Prospect, and Molyneux adds, 'the upper portion was subsequently blown down in a gale of wind'. He offers no date but on an engraving inscribed 'Burton-on-Trent 1779', mainly an interesting depiction of part of old Burton bridge, the roof lines of the town are consistently level except for the Parish Church tower. This suggests that our high building was damaged between 1732 and 1779. Molyneux next refers to Hicklin's brewery 'at our rear of the Crown Inn, now the shop and premises of Mr. Birch near the Bank'. This was a small brewery belonging to Benjamin Hicklin, who was also landlord of the Crown. It operated from 1845 until 1860. Historian H.J. Wain later places the Crown 'on a site now occupied by Lloyds Bank'.

In 1851 the Burton Union Bank, as it then was, was still in the Market Place. Brewer Hicklin was listed as landlord of the 'Old Crown' but it was no longer listed as a posting inn. About this time there was a soup kitchen in the vicinity, which could well have been temporary use of vacant premises prior to demolition. The bank stood on its new site by 1857, so it would seem that the Crown finally disappeared in the mid-1850s.

None of this positively identifies the Crown with Buck's ornamental building or with 'an adjoining house' as Molyneux suggests. It is not easy, though, to consider such a structure as being a house and perhaps the matter can be resolved if we acknowledge that the Buck brothers were highly skilled and accurate artists and draughtsmen. Look through a magnifier at this tall building and there is little doubt that the top of the structure resembles – entirely appropriately – an ornamental crown!

Nine

One for the Album

The scenes assembled for this chapter would originally have been kept for their family associations or for their general interest. There must still be a storehouse of local and social history in old photograph albums and one would like to feel that they are being carefully preserved and, hopefully, that as much information as possible is also recorded, so that they retain meaning and significance for future owners and for historians.

The title 'Alderman' is of ancient origin, being an Anglo-Saxon elder. It was bestowed on senior members of councils in recognition of services rendered. On 20 April 1949 Alderman William Hutson JP additionally received the Honorary Freedom of the County Borough. Presiding at the ceremony is the Mayor, Councillor John Jones J.P. with the Town Clerk, W. Bailey Chapman (right). William Hutson is chiefly recalled now by the school named after him but he was prominent in local affairs from 1920, Mayor in 1932 and Alderman from 1939. He died in 1950.

William Molyneux F.G.S, F.R.Hist. S. published his book *The History, Waters and Breweries of Burton-on-Trent* in 1869. It remains a valuable source of local information. Born in Oxfordshire in 1824 he came to Burton as mining engineer to the Marquis of Anglesey, to whom he dedicated the book. A prominent geologist, he was a co-founder of the Natural History and Archaeological Society and the advocate for the flood embankment to the south of the town, which has proved so invaluable during periods of flooding. He died in South Africa in 1882.

Mr Simnett didn't have far to paddle to take this photograph, being already established in the area. The October 1875 flood was the second serious inundation that year, following one in July. It led to the erection in 1880 of the flood embankment advocated by William Molyneux. The building on Guild Street corner (on the left) was the old police station (no familiar dome in the distance until 1910). The 1875 floods were reported to have caused damage estimated at £100,000, a vast sum in those days.

This delightful image was taken at Carver's Rocks, a local beauty spot favoured for picnics and by walkers. It would be hard to find a more charming reminder of a visit since the photographer seems to have captured a completely spontaneous moment. Foremark reservoir has now greatly altered the landscape here and brought water board formality along with visitor facilities, but it still remains a popular place for a countryside outing.

Another favourite local resort was a stroll by the Trent on the fringes of Drakelow Park where this snapshot photograph was taken in 1925. The changes in fashion are of interest. Up to a dozen years previously everyone, both men and women, wore a hat and usually dressed very formally, often in black, even for a summer afternoon stroll in the countryside. It was not to be long before scenes around here were greatly altered and Drakelow mansion had been demolished.

Burton Post Office cricket club did not allow sporting prowess to interfere with routine. In 1909 letters at twenty sub-offices and thirty-five wall boxes were cleared at least six times daily, often with same day delivery. Letters were delivered from early morning until nine o'clock at night, and all mail was sure of delivery anywhere by next day. The boxes on the station platform and Station Bridge were cleared nineteen times every twenty-four hours, so that a postcard could be sent saying: 'Just arrived Burton 10:30. Home in Leek at 7:15'. Further comments would seem to be superfluous!

Although in itself this was hardly a serious occasion, the photograph serves as a recollection of the earlier days of Burton Rugby Club. Founded in 1870 it achieved distinction in the later years of the century. Photographs of the old teams are elusive but without doubt this group will include some of those who distinguished themselves in Victorian times when the club twice won the Midland Counties cup, defeated the first Maori tourists and had Frank Evershed in the England side. The club played on Peel Croft from 1889.

NEWTON SOLNEY F.C.

Newton Solney Football Club was formed in 1932 and played in the Burton and District League in the 1930s. Back row, left to right: A. Judd (chairman), A. Thorpe, H. Birch, J. Brown, J. Bullions, H. Rees, W. Hoar. Front row: L. Mason, A. Carlton, H. Brown, F. Dawson, C. Palmer, L. Beckley (captain). This is one of the series of photocards of local teams issued by the Ardath Tobacco Company.

Used as their Christmas card, this is the Cotton family outside No. 11 Newton Road in 1905. Like his father Henry Cotton senior, his son Henry was also an engine driver. On 8 October 1919, Burton-Ashby tram No. 19 ran backwards down Bearwood Hill and if any of the Cotton family saw it coming straight for this house, it must have been a moment of panic. Thankfully the tram rounded the start of a severe left-hand curve before overturning into the garden of River House, just clear of Nos. 10 and 11, the first two houses in Newton Road. The accident caused two deaths and many injuries.

A newspaper correspondent recently suggested there could be economy in paper used for envelopes, apart from simplicity and timesaving, if Christmas cards were of postcard format. This card, posted on Christmas Eve (delivered Christmas Day!) shows Tutbury well in advance on this idea. The design however is hardly seasonal, and it is probable that the publisher used it with various messages. Christmas postcards had limited popularity, perhaps because for eleven months shops would have carried idle stock.

Lord Burton's final benefaction to the town was St Chad's church in Hunter Street (architect, G.F. Bodley) consecrated by the Bishop of Lichfield on 6 July 1910. This was a new parish (1903) and Hunter Street itself was then newly built. Umbrellas indicate that the weather was unkind but continuous rain did not deter a packed congregation for the impressive church ceremony; while large crowds assembled outside under flags and bunting. The Dowager Lady Burton entertained principal guests to tea in the parish room.

The flourishing choir of St Aidan's church, Shobnall, in 1909. Built as a chapel-of-ease to St John's, a new parish was formed in 1916. Centre is Revd J.G. Jones and there are six members of the Appleby family who were stalwart parishioners. Three were coopers living on Shobnall Road, while Denis Stuart's *County Borough History* records how a Mrs Appleby of Forest Road, a midwife, might be tapped on the shoulder during service, leaving the choir boys to speculate on whose turn it was next.

The late Victorian and Edwardian period saw a fashion for things Chinese and Japanese. Ornamental items of every description became the vogue and the craze was reflected in plays and musicals with oriental settings such as *A Chinese Honeymoon*, *Chu Chin Chow* and *The Mousmé*. Japanese themes in particular became popular at bazaars and social events, with appropriate costume, as seen here with the Japanese choir at Newhall Church bazaar in 1909. When Burton Opera House opened in 1902, the 'Geisha Room' was specially designed for lady patrons.

The location of this interesting photograph by J.S. Simnett is not identifiable but it was obviously taken when Church Army passed through the Burton area on their route march. These began just after the First World War when a party left a cathedral city (sent off by an Archbishop or Bishop), arriving at a seaside resort for a Summer Beach Mission. Marches began each year from a different city to a different resort and mission visits would have been arranged for villages and towns en route. A retired officer suggests around 1928 for this particular march. Those taking part were students from the Church Army 'Wilson Carlile College of Evangelism' at Sheffield, and Church Army officers.

Route marches are no longer featured but the seaside beach missions still continu – in 1998 for example there was attendance at Bridlington, Blackpool, Yarmouth, Lowestoft, Clacton and the North Wales resorts. Church Army still thrives as a Society of Evangelists within the Anglican community, working with children and young people, the elderly and the homeless, as well as assisting in the establishment of new churches and the promotion of community evangelism in various spheres.

In previous books we have dealt with the aeronautical aspects of Burton's noted Aviation meeting of 1910. There was also a significant social side to the week's activities. The Corporation provided an official hospitality tent presided over by the Mayor for the entertainment of important visitors. One such group is pictured here. The Mayor at the time of the event was Thomas Jenkins, an architect. His work included the Electric Theatre, the upper façade of which survives in High Street (dated 1910) though unfortunately minus its original decorative features.

A Wetmore Road school photograp, c. 1902. It is of high quality (by a London photographer) and shows the wearing apparel of these young Burtonians to full advantage. They appear well dressed, although this school served a working-class neighbourhood. Perhaps advance notice meant that Sunday best could be worn. The medal sported by the boy in the centre could commemorate the coronation of King Edward VII. The school building is typical of its period and there will be no looking out of those windows – even the bottom row of glass is frosted!

When Burton Infirmary was voluntarily supported, the South Derbyshire area regularly staged elaborate galas and parades in aid of funds. This is a typical decorated wagon from the grand procession at the Moira and Donisthorpe Hospital Parade of 1914. These members of the Moira Choral Society serve as a reminder of the musical traditions of the area and of the high quality of church, chapel and other choirs.

An early Edwardian photograph of surgeons and nursing staff of Burton Infirmary. After rebuilding, completed in 1899, there was a complement of seventy-two beds, but fever patients were now admitted to the new Isolation Hospital at Outwoods. A new Casualty, Out Patients and Dispensary were built on the New Street frontage. There were minor problems as recorded in minutes. A toilet for out patients attracted local small boys who, when warned off after increased supervision, made use of the entrance porch instead!

Burton had Sunday schools by the early nineteenth century but growth was most rapid from around1860, when the local Sunday school Union was formed with 1047 scholars and 152 teachers from seven schools. The Jubilee Celebrations of September 1913 could claim 3694 scholars and 461 teachers from twenty-six schools. There were events in the Town Hall and in King Edward Place (seen here) where crowds attend a service, the platform being a dray provided by coal merchant Mr C. Spalding. Scholars received badges; long service awards were presented to teachers.

Lady members of George Street Chapel among the team responsible for the extensive Refreshment Department at the three-day Grand Bazaar of 1908. In the rear row are Mrs Binns, Mrs Mason and Mrs Bagnall. On the left is Mrs Warr, and seated centre and right, Mrs V. Tresise and Mrs Lambrick. Bazaar refreshment stalls were all-important and I still recall my hilarity at similar events in my own youth when the 'Home made refreshments' were always located under a flowing painted wall text rather unfortunately inscribed: 'Prepare To Meet Your God'.

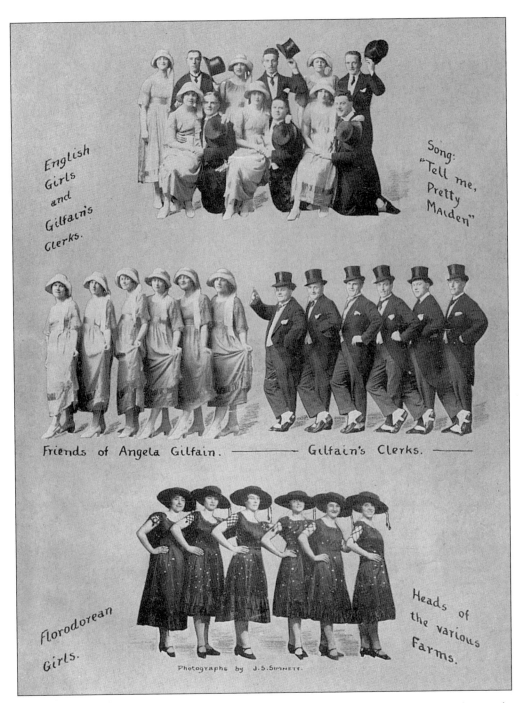

English Girls and Gilfain's Clerks.

Song: "Tell me, Pretty Maiden"

Friends of Angela Gilfain. ———— Gilfain's Clerks. ————

Florodorean Girls.

Heads of the various Farms.

Photographs by J.S.Simnett.

For 1926 Burton Operatic Society's choice was the popular Leslie Stuart musical comedy *Florodora* – very much a contemporary piece featuring dancing, romance and humour; and reflecting the taste, style and costumes of the twenties. Prior to 1914, Gilbert and Sullivan had predominated. The 'New' post-war Society staged a range of popular shows including *The Geisha, The Rebel Maid, Tom Jones* and *Dorothy* – the latter, played twice, was the Society's farewell to the Opera House which closed in 1934.

Staff of the *Burton Daily Mail* photographed during a rather formal outing to the east-coast, shortly before the First World War. Everyone has dressed up for the occasion though, with a generous array of the fashionable straw boaters as a concession to informality. The photographer was local, listing branches at Mablethorpe and Skegness, the latter resort the favourite for a Burton excursion.

Girls from St Modwen's Roman Catholic school on Burton station, probably in the early 1930s. Backpacks were obviously not yet in vogue and there is a range of handbags on show including the popular attaché case and a Gladstone bag. The latter was often associated with doctors or nurses producing their stethoscopes from 'the little black bag'. Having to carry bags must have been an encumbrance on school trips. By the clothes being worn this was possibly not a summer outing.

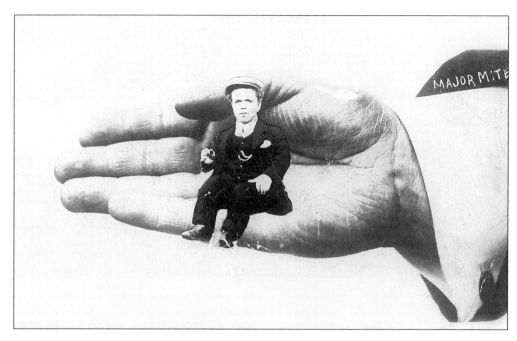

The Dorette series of postcards by Siddals of Newhall provides some fine local scenes and local history records. Siddals remains something of an enigma, however, little firm information coming to hand about his career. This card too is something of an oddity. A dwarf calling himself 'General Mite' (under two feet in height when age seventeen) was exhibited in London in 1881. This card dates from the early 1900s. Was a demoted 'Major Mite' still making appearances, possibly at Newhall wakes, for Siddals to try his hand at trick photography?

This Victorian post box is still in use on Tatenhill Common. It becomes a relic of historic local interest when one realises that it has been in continuous use during three centuries. Any threat to replace it deserves to be resisted since few examples of VR boxes now remain. A mail van driver collecting from the surviving VR box in Elms Road, Stapenhill, could only cite two others in the Ashbourne area and one at the Acorn Inn.

It must have been a calm day when the photographer achieved this image with its extremely clear reflection. Posted in, and addressed to, Burton in 1906, the scene is the Trent and Mersey canal at one of several possible points where canal and railway are in close proximity, there being a signal box in view. The steam launch, called *Mimosa*, is of unusual design and while it could have become a pleasure craft, one authority suggests that it many have been a canal service or maintenance vessel.

Written from Oak Street, Burton, the accompanying message says: 'I have sent you a photograph of the old shop on wheels'. The donor of this postcard remembered his grandmother's Friday night call with assorted household items and a regular delivery of paraffin for the Valor stove, which provided extra heat (and the menace of smoke from an uneven wick). It was also for the lamp, which hung up at night in the outside (and only) toilet, for light and to prevent the tank from freezing in winter.

WINSHILL.   HIGH STREET.   PARISH CHURCH.   TRENT BRIDGE.   BURTON-ON-TRENT.   CHERRY ORCHARD.

Old albums invariably contained examples of multi-view postcards which were produced in large numbers and were much favoured, no doubt because one card provided a range of impressions of a particular locality. Drawbacks were that with cards of inferior quality small pictures could be indistinct; while some publishers incorporated so many scenes that they were too small to be of much interest. A good photographic card however, especially if magnified, could convey a really worthwhile record of four or five local views. This is one excellent example from the studio of F.W. Scarratt of Derby, a first-rate photographer. Note how his lightweight motorcycle, and that of his companion, are included to give life to scenes which, in themselves, were often taken by Scarratt from an unusual viewpoint, adding to their appeal.

It is surprising how this one multi-view card actually supplements several other pictures in this volume. The Bearwood Hill scene (top left) shows the view of No. 11 Newton Road (page 67) would have had of the gradient down which the runaway tram ran out of control. The bottom left scene perfectly illustrates how the single line tram track was tight to one side of Trent Bridge before widening took place and the track was doubled. The High Street scene shows the demolished George Hotel (page 19) in relation to other High Street premises; and the Cherry Orchard scene, with its immaculate lawn, emphasises the comments made accompanying our image (on page 44).

Ten

Sir Oswald's Loaf

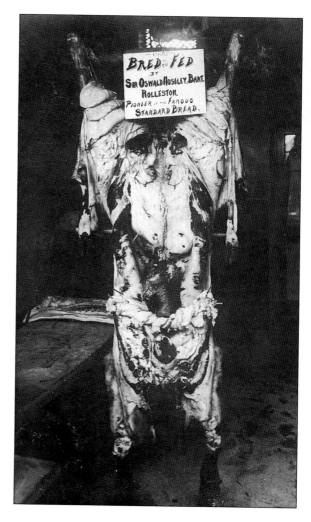

Sir Oswald Mosley, fourth Bart (1848-1915) was the last member of the family to be actively involved in local affairs before their Rolleston estate was sold and the family home, Rolleston Hall, was largely demolished in the 1920s. Sir Oswald is usually associated with such public events as the unveiling of the Lord Burton statue in 1911 when he addressed the crowds assembled on that auspicious occasion. It was in the same year, however, that Sir Oswald embarked on an intriguing campaign which was taken up nationally from humble beginnings based on Rolleston and Burton.

This story, largely forgotten today, was revived by a somewhat grotesque picture found in a postcard album alongside such conventional views as Skegness Pier and Buckingham Palace. The notice tells us that this is the carcass of a calf 'bred and fed by Sir Oswald Mosley' and then adds 'Pioneer of the famous Standard read'. It is dated Christmas 1911.

The full story is best told by Sir Oswald himself in the course of a full page feature in the *London Evening News* of 22 February, 1911. Firstly there is a long leader article proclaiming that the demand for bread containing the maximum of nutriment for the minimum bulk has been answered by the loaf now widely recommended and receiving full support from the government, hospitals, the medical profession and many other bodies. The theme is that 'a standard should be fixed for the nutritive value of what is sold as bread (like the standard recently enforced by law for milk). In view of the inferior qualities of white bread commonly sold, legislation should make it compulsory that all bread should be made from unadulterated wheat flour containing at least eighty per cent of the whole wheat including the germ and semolina'.

Sir Oswald then takes up the story. He had produced a small pamphlet originally intended for his own area around Rolleston but the *Daily Mail* had obtained a copy and within weeks it had become an issue of national interest. Sir Oswald stated that for some thirty years he had enjoyed the pure flour stone-ground for him by Messrs Greensmith of the Old Mills, Burton. They extracted the outer bran only, which went for animal food, leaving the whole of the rest of the wheat grain in the flour. This was used by Sir Oswald's village baker, and every loaf produced was of the same consistency and quality.

Advertisements surrounding the article showed that many London bakeries were already supplying the pure flour to make Standard Bread. Also of interest is the advertisement for the Rolleston portable brick lined oven, which quotes Sir Oswald as saying: 'Undoubtedly the old brick ovens with stick fires inside are the best'. He recalled in the newspaper article how, as a youngster, he had taken bags of wheat to the local miller, watched it being stone-ground and had then carried the flour home and watched the baking of the bread straight away in the brick oven in the kitchen. Thus was Rolleston in the national spotlight in 1911, thanks to Sir Oswald's campaign for Standard Bread.

Watching the Hounds at Rolleston 48-12.

Here Rolleston villagers are gathered near the Spread Eagle to watch a meet of the Meynell Hunt. In the background can be seen the premises of William Whetton, listed in the 1911 directory as grocer and baker. Sir Oswald refers to his village baker so presumably this is where Rolleston's Standard Bread was baked for many years before the campaign assumed national recognition. Note the white-coated delivery boy with his basket among the spectators.

Sadly Greensmith's mill closed in May 1991 and its splendid machinery was broken up. This historic protected building now awaits future development. Much of it dates from c. 1745, but the site almost certainly dates back to pre-Norman times and it was subsequently the mill that ground malt and corn for Burton Abbey. This is a view in its Edwardian hey-day when its name and reputation became widely known through Sir Oswald Mosley's publicity.

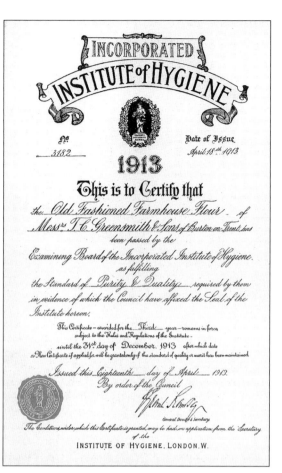

Certificate of Hygiene issued in 1913 for Greensmith's 'Old Fashioned Farmhouse Flour'. Printed on the back appeared: 'T.G. Greensmith & Sons of Burton upon Trent proudly call attention to the fact that they were the original millers of the flour approved and recommended by Sir Oswald Mosley, Bt'.

Plainly not averse to publicity for himself, Sir Oswald allowed his photograph to appear on the address side of Greensmith's business envelopes, the back of which also advised that their farmhouse flour was now supplied to all the leading hydros.

Eat Bread made from Greensmith's
OLD FASHIONED FARMHOUSE FLOUR

As approved by and supplied to

SIR OSWALD MOSLEY, Bart.
and the Leading Hydros.

All the Best *Bakers sell it.*

Eleven

Volunteers

On Easter Monday 1861 there were reviews and sham fights by the Burton Rifle Volunteers. This local unit, the 98th Regiment of Foot, was to become the 2nd Battalion, North Staffordshire Regiment, in 1881.

'There was an impressive turn-out of the war-like youth of our town, though the weather was not as fine as had been prophesised by our milkman, who can see signs and tokens over Waterloo Clump and knows when a shower is coming up out of Tatenhill hole.' *The Burton upon Trent Times* reporter then continued his account: 'At one o'clock the Market Place was crowded with the 'Greys' and spectators. The corps, headed by the band, proceeded through the town accompanied by a large crowd and soon found themselves on the Newton Road over ankles in dirt. But with a steady if heavy march they reached the field selected for the day's operation. Shortly, the scarlet Garibaldian suits (red shirt, white trousers) of the fine lads of Repton school came in view and took up their ground under their instructors. The various exercises and movements were now admirably gone through and the bayonet exercise excited universal admiration...there was plenty of blank cartridge fired off in file firing, firing from the square and volley firing'.

Local society attended on foot and in carriages to watch, including Dr Pears, the memorable Repton headmaster. After the review there was a march to the residence of Mr Worthington (Newton Park) where officers and visitors were entertained indoors. For the Volunteers there were tables on the lawn with 'pork pies in rank and file' and Burton beer, the band playing during the repast. After a line-up and cheers, the troops returned to Burton behind the band. The Repton lads had marched straight back – 'owing to the lightness of their dress' according to the press, though an old Reptonian recorded that when beer was served they were promptly 'doubled off'. They dined together at the school that evening under the presidency of Dr Pears. Postscript from the following week's newspaper: Volunteer Rifle Corps. 'Edinburgh Life Assurance Company requires no extra premium for Military Service of any description within the United Kingdom'.

The opportunity for much more serious business came in 1899 when local volunteers were called upon following the outbreak of the Boer War. As in many of Britain's colonial engagements the difficulties of the task were underestimated so that the first months saw British defeats and public pessimism at home. British forces were shut up in Ladysmith, Kimberley and Mafeking, which were not relieved until reinforcements, many of them volunteers, were dispatched. The relief of Mafeking in May 1900 caused wild celebration. 'When Shall Their Glory Fade' and 'Britain's Most Heroic Defence Ends In Triumph' were *Daily Express* headlines, typical of public relief and concern for the troops. In Burton a procession round the town was organised within two days.

In a hastily written popular song, a new verb, to 'maffick' came into being:

> 'Mother may I go and maffick,
> Run about and hinder traffic?'

> (*Oxford English Dictionary*: Maffick-To exult riotously).

The war, in fact, continued for another two years, the 'clearing up' proving difficult, and it was May 1902 before peace was declared. In 1910 General Botha, the Boer leader, became the first Prime Minister of the new British dominion – the Union of South Africa. The return of North Staffs Volunteers was the occasion for an enthusiastic 'Welcome Home'. On 20 May 1902, with bands playing, they marched from the Town Hall to the Parish Church for a service of thanksgiving. Big crowds repeated the fervour shown in the early days of the war when groups of volunteers had paraded before leaving the town.

This fine crowd scene demonstrates the enormous enthusiasm of Burtonians for parades and the desire to pay tribute to the troops. The procession is imminent with the Station Bridge and Station Street, providing a classic example of 'mafficking'. The horse cab conveys its own message; the Station Hotel barrow tries to make progress; while the luckiest spectators enjoy a grandstand view from above the low shop fronts near Mosley Street. Local Yeomanry Volunteers returned a few weeks later.

Another large crowd greets the Volunteers' arrival in the Market Place. Nothing of this scene remains today – Ellis's small corner shop (replaced 1908), Jackson the jeweller, Lakin's oyster rooms and the grocery of F.W. Bass, all are long gone. Facing the camera was the Burton Club, Walker Brothers' drapery, Oakden's grocery, with the top of the White Hart just visible. The band played *Home, Sweet Home*, *The British Grenadiers*, *Hearts of Oak* and *Soldiers of the King*. The overseas contingent proudly held aloft a Boer flag captured at Johannesburg.

Prior to departure after the thanksgiving service, the troops wait alongside carriages drawn up for principal dignitaries. There is a good view of Worthington's Royal Oak as it then appeared. As customary in those days everyone has headgear; not the flat pill-box type hat worn by the constabulary at this time (bottom left). It should be recorded that ten Burton women volunteered for hospital work in South Africa and Burtonians also served in units other than the North Staffs and Yeomanry.

Here, re-mustering is still going on. The centre group comprises councillors in their morning coats and top hats. At the front, wearing his chain of office, is the Mayor, J.R. Morris, head of a cooperage in Horninglow Street. The balcony of The Man In The Moon provided grandstand viewing for many public occasions, but every vantage point is occupied. The troops returned for a Town Hall lunch via the High Street, Horninglow Street, Derby Street, Byrkley Street and Waterloo Street, giving other parts of town a chance to cheer the march.

Queen's Own Royal Regiment.

Anglesey "G" Troop Ball.

Lady Patroness Mrs Hugh S. Charrington.

The Committee request the pleasure of the company of

Trooper Eason

at the Town Hall, Burton-on-Trent, on Friday evening Feb 12th 1897.
Dancing 9 to 3. The Band of the Regiment will be in attendance.
(Bandmaster, J. Gladman)

Gentlemen's Tickets 12/6.   *Ladies Tickets 8/6.*
Double Tickets (Lady & Gentleman) 21/- including Supper.

Application for Tickets to be made to Sergt R. Peach, Branstone Road, Burton-on-Trent.
The number of Tickets issued will be strictly limited.   *Joint Hon. Secs* {*Sergt R. Peach.*
An early answer is requested.   *T.J. Bindley.*

The other local volunteer unit was the Anglesey Troop of the Queen's Own Royal Regiment. The Staffordshire Yeomanry originated in 1794, receiving its new title in 1838. We are reminded that this was a cavalry unit by the invitation to Trooper Eason to attend the grand ball at Burton Town Hall in February 1897, illustrating the social side of military life. Soon afterwards local Yeomanry volunteers became part of the Imperial Yeomanry, some serving in South Africa.

A range of dress uniforms is displayed in this group of NCOs and other ranks of the Staffordshire Yeomanry. The house behind them has been identified as Ashfield House, residence of Alderman Morris, Burton's mayor, and it seems likely that this photograph was taken when he hosted an informal gathering of local Yeomanry Volunteers returning from Boer War Service who arrived back later than the North Staffs Volunteers.

Repton School Rifle Corps was newly formed when it took part in the 1861 review. It lasted until 1875, cadets drilling twice weekly under a sergeant instructor. Subsequently the Officers' Training Corps (OTC) was inaugurated in schools and universities in 1909 and became very active, especially with the outbreak of war in 1914. This scene records the 1910 school field day. By 1918 some in the picture would be among the 355 old Reptonians who gave their lives.

The Boer War demonstrated an urgent need for army reorganisation. After the establishment of the Territorial Force in 1907 (the Territorial Army from 1921), Volunteers and Yeomanry became part of a new voluntary force, training locally and attending a fortnight's annual camp for exercises with other units. The scene shows the Staffordshire Volunteer camp of 1907 at Conway. North Wales was a regular location with local units photographed at Towyn and Prestatyn.

No account is known of Barton Athletes Volunteer Force seen here around 1915 drilling (with staves) on the cricket field (Walton and Drakelow Halls in background). Steve Gardner (*Life and Times in Barton*) records a Barton committee staging athletic sports between 1885 and 1911, and this group could have evolved from that source in the early war years for fitness training and drill. The postcard says: 'This is the 'Esprit de Corps de Swank' or the knobs of Burton (sic) doing their little bit', so it probably drew volunteers from around the area.

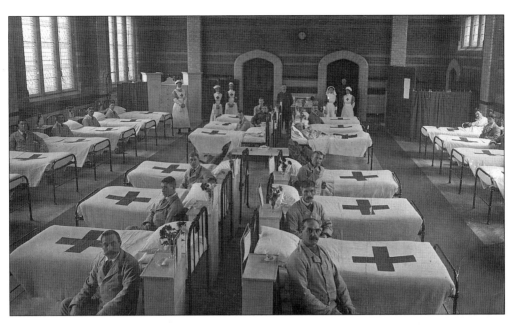

Many women volunteered their services in a variety of ways during both world wars. Red Cross volunteers manned hospitals established during World War One in Burton Town Hall and in St Paul's Institute, the location featured in this photograph. It also serves as a record of the interior of this hall, popular for many local events and activities prior to demolition in 1979.

Many other women replaced men in factories and breweries around the town. Here Bass ale is being carefully packed with straw in wooden crates to be dispatched overseas. The crate nearest Simnett's camera is marked for France and holds six dozen half-bottles.

Beer and tobacco usually went together as far as the troops were concerned and there was much voluntary local activity in fund raising and organization to supply cigarettes, tobacco (and other comforts, like gloves) for the forces. In Burton Uncle Jack's Smokes Fund operated through the *Burton Daily Mail* and the Tobacco Committee in the photograph, dated 1914, functioned in the area raising money for similar provision.

In an earlier collection we paid tribute to Lily Thomas, founder and secretary of the Burton Prisoners of War Fund (1915-18). 25,700 parcels were sent out under the Red Cross scheme, hundreds of men benefiting. We included a photograph of Lily Thomas with repatriated prisoners, who were honoured at civic receptions and thanksgiving services. Here she appears with a group of youngsters recalling local fund raising support, probably the children's fête organized at Horninglow, which raised £250.

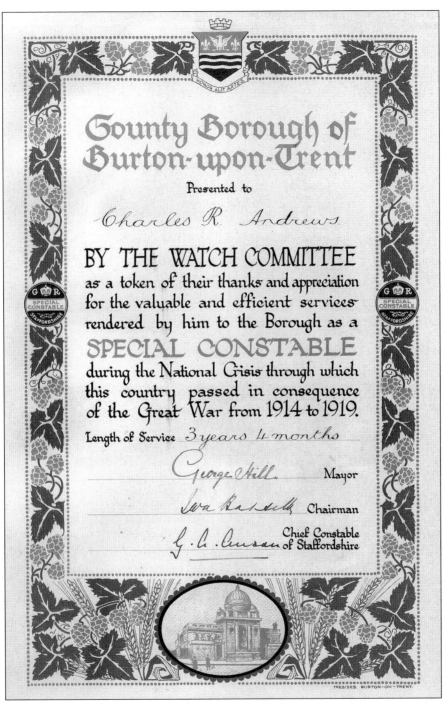

County Borough of Burton-upon-Trent

Presented to

Charles R. Andrews

BY THE WATCH COMMITTEE

as a token of their thanks and appreciation for the valuable and efficient services rendered by him to the Borough as a

SPECIAL CONSTABLE

during the National Crisis through which this country passed in consequence of the Great War from 1914 to 1919.

Length of Service *3 years 4 months*

George Hill. Mayor

Ivor Rawsell Chairman

G. C. Ausan Chief Constable of Staffordshire

TRESISES. BURTON-ON-TRENT.

A decorative certificate (originally framed) was presented to Mr C.R. Andrews of Belvedere Road, in recognition of his services as a special constable during the First World War. The motif for the frame incorporates barley and hops and a view of the domed court house, of which Pevsner commented: 'It might be a variety theatre.' Locals dubbed it Moss's mosque, Mr William Moss being Superintendent of Police at the time.

In previous books we have shown the unveiling of Burton War Memorial in August 1922 by Lord Dartmouth; and also the temporary cenotaph erected in the market place for 1921, a memorial service being held in the Parish church in 1919 and 1920. This scene shows wreaths being inspected after the 1922 ceremony. The War Memorial commemorated some 1,300 men whose names were inscribed on panels in the Town Hall foyer by the Peace Celebration Committee in 1920, World War Two names being subsequently added.

Local villages also commemorated the fallen, sometimes with a war memorial, as at Barton. Rolleston however decided on a lych (lich) gate, duly erected by Bridgemans of Lichfield for £310, raised by public subscription. It was dedicated by the Bishop of Lichfield serving as a memorial for those who died in both world wars, an additional tablet being added after World War Two. A lych gate was intended as a shelter for coffin and mourners awaiting being conducted into church, the old word 'Lich' meaning a dead body.

We can represent all those honoured by the War Memorial with this photograph of Private S.C. Deacon of the Nottinghamshire and Derbyshire Regiment. Private Deacon was commemorated by his family through a large framed certificate which, sadly, found its way eventually into a second-hand shop. Twenty by sixteen inches, it proved too large to reproduce without loss of detail, but removal from the frame revealed the photograph. The certificate is a much more elaborate version of that for Special Constable Andrews (on page 91), showing a highly coloured Town Hall, the County Borough Arms and a variety of symbols in a design by C.A.F. Bernard.

For gootness sake go back ! Here kom der NOTTS. & DERBYS.

This type of comic card enjoyed popularity in the early days of the war with talk of 'all over by Christmas'. Many Burton and South Derbyshire men served with the Notts and Derbys. As the war dragged on, of course, the humour lost its impact and the card became rather a sick joke. After the 6th North Staffs, the Notts and Derbys list on the Town Hall memorial boards is probably the next longest toll of local casualties.

93

In World War Two almost everyone, young or old, became a volunteer in one capacity or another. There was auxiliary nursing and the auxiliary fire service; the many branches of air raid precautions and rescue work; as well as such duties as fire watching, the observer corps or the WVS – all quite apart from varied occupations involved in essential war work. Additionally nearly everyone answered the famous call 'Dig for Victory', taking advantage of double summer time for work in garden or allotment on top of all other commitments.

No voluntary service account would be complete without reference to the Home Guard, immortalised in *Dad's Army*. It soon became well organised and efficient, and within three months the Local Defence Volunteers of May 1940, numbered 1,300,000. In 1941 the restructured 8th (Burton) Battalion had a strength of 2,500. Representing them is Sgt A. Lester of 'A' Company. Known as 'Pop', he served until the battalion stood-down. Never late and never missing a parade, this old timer received the Certificate of Good Service.

Twelve
Sporting a Penny

Reflecting on picking up a penny off the carpet on the day the new European currency was launched, it caused one to regret that it has now become such a sad and devalued little coin, of toy money size, the first to escape when holes appear in trouser pockets, as if ashamed of its lost status.

From once being a silver coin, with a long, proud history, earning a prominent place in everyday language and phraseology, the change from 1d (from the Roman *denarius*) to 1p on decimalisation was an early stab at our threatened national inheritance. How the country appreciated the penny post of 1840; how collectors sought the penny black stamp; the penny bank would take deposits of as little as a penny. Children relished the feel of the substantial old bronze coin when choosing their penn'orth of sweets or making up their minds in Burton's penny bazaar. It was a penny for the guy or the old man's hat; to say nothing of the quotes and proverbs based on it – 'In for a penny, in for a pound', 'A penny for your thoughts', and all the rest of them. And of course you went to spend a penny!

This delightful advertising card from Fry's (artist, Tom Browne) shows a small girl clutching her penny while envious friends watch through the window – 'See their eyes as she buys Fry's.' Similar little local sweet shops sold many a penny chocolate bar on pocket money day. Offa (757-796) was the first English ruler to strike a silver penny and as he was king of Mercia it is probable that our area was one of the first to see his 'new penny' (novus denarius).

Almost forgotten now are the penny readings which became a favourite form of entertainment – amateur, voluntary and often parochial – it which readings and songs provided a simple social occasion. Behind their organization, mainly from the early 1860s until the Edwardian era, they combined a well-meant desire to educate as well as to entertain. They became very popular locally.

Let me introduce Mr David Lewis (1823-1885) founder of Lewis's stores and, at the time of his death, 'the largest retail merchant in the world' and noted as entrepreneur and benefactor. In front of me as I write is a copy of *Lewis's Penny Readings*, a neat bound book containing 130 pages of 'Selections from the Best Poets, Prose Writers and Speakers' and published by Lewis's 'for the nominal sum of one PENNY'. Unearthed in Burton, I suspect it formed a basis for some of our local penny readings.

This subsidised volume was Mr. Lewis's philanthropic contribution to what he plainly saw as a Good Cause. 'In issuing these 'Penny Readings' we are actuated to put into circulation a sound, amusing and instructive kind of reading, which shall be within the reach of every section of the community. It is earnestly hoped that this book may specially touch the GROWING BOYS AND YOUTHS of our large commercial centres; one of our principle reasons for publishing it being to supersede by a healthy class of literature those sensational novels and tales, whose heroes are too frequently thieves, and whose so-called gallant exploits raise an unworthy desire for emulation in the minds of the ill-trained, untaught youths who delight in such pernicious works'. It was also hoped that it would prove attractive for home reading.

Whether the contents, not greatly relieved by light heartedness, would appeal to those who were so sternly reproached in the preface may be open to doubt. The real hope of course was that here might be useful source material for Penny Readings to replace the Penny Dreadfuls, which many of them presumably read; and the Penny Gaffs, which offered the lowest form of theatrical entertainment. Burton had its share of small companies who erected a tent to stage one-night selections of melodrama, admission one penny.

For the readings themselves Shakespeare and Dickens were widely used, especially *The Death of Little Nell*, a guaranteed tearjerker; and extracts from *A Christmas Carol*, not limited to inclusion only at Christmas. Poems often featured included *Excelsior, The Inchcape Rock, The Village Blacksmith, The Jackdaw of Rheims* and *The Wreck of the Hesperus*. I will quote from just one of Mr Lewis's sterner prose extracts.

'Look at this glass of water in my hand! Did you ever feel the tongue dry, the lips parched, the throat feverish, and then, bringing a goblet filled with pure water to your lips, do you remember the sensation as it trickled over the tongue and gurgled down you throat? Was it not a luxury? Surely it is a luxury to quench thirst in pure spring water. Here is a beverage brewed for us by our Heavenly Father – brewed too in beautiful places and not amid the smoky fires, the horrid stench and rank corruption that fester around the distillery or brewhouse?' I suspect this was one item not offered to Burton audiences!

Perhaps it was a shortage of suitable or talented readers (press reports were often critical) which led to introducing Penny Concerts, which became almost entirely musical. Another variant was the introduction of magic lantern slides, already widely used by lecturers. Very successful were song slides when the words, with appropriate, highly coloured pictures, appeared on a screen allowing a repeat performance of the song with the audience joining in. Many of these slide sets were produced by Bamforths of Holmfirth who later published many of them as sets of penny postcards.

You might expect that these simple, cheap entertainments, often arranged by chapels, churches or the YMCA, would have been quite straightforward and non-controversial. It is revealing therefore to read contemporary accounts of events.

In January 1866 'The Town Hall was again densely packed and many were compelled to go away unable to obtain accommodation. The chairman expressed approval of such gatherings feeling that they were calculated to do much good'. He was then answered in the press by 'One Who Occasionally Sports A Penny', who wrote: 'While supporting complaint about the want of accommodation at the so-called Penny Readings in the town, I cannot imagine that it is right that the Town Hall should be filled with 'Threepenny Touches' while others, for whose improvement our Christian friends tell us these meetings are designed, are left (if they can enter the room at all) to stand round the door, crowded and much inconvenienced. I don't think the smallness of the building should be made an excuse for this and it appears to me that YMCA, while ostensibly endeavouring to benefit working people, are in reality fast getting rich by exclusion of those they pretend to improve'.

At the next meeting the chairman criticised 'those who, often without abilities to please or amuse, unjustifiably sneer at those who make sacrifices for the benefit of a good cause and the improvement of their less fortunate brethren'. The final session of that winter was to be in aid of a new Burton Dispensary Building Fund so the admission price was raised. Correspondents now reprimanded the YMCA for not devoting more of the proceeds of previous readings to charity funds other than their own and 'healthy opposition' was promised for the next season. Perhaps as a distraction from these unfortunate bickerings, one writer, signing himself 'A Victim', tried to divert attention from tired feet through having to stand to the consequences of arriving early and having a long sit: 'Allow me to suggest the desirableness of having the town hall seats cushioned with some cheap stuff. In these days of spring seats and easy chairs it is a great hardship to sit for two mortal hours on a bare plank...'

However most penny readings provided simple pleasure for many people thanks to those volunteers who contributed with the best of intentions. Let us leave the topic before I am accused of being a Penny-a-Liner. Contributors to local papers were sometimes paid a penny a line, which possibly explains some of that lengthy, verbose reporting of the past. Now it is just another of those old, fascinating penny-phrases that have disappeared, like today's little penny, through the hole in the pocket. There is something to be said though in praise of this undistinguished little coin – at least it still displays the old historical words: One Penny!

An early Edwardian Penny Concert, where the programme has become almost entirely musical with just one reading and one monologue to recall the beginnings of these occasions as Penny Readings. When they first became fashionable, Burton Musical Society emphasised their superior status by announcing (1867) the first of a series of Shilling Concerts (one shilling being twelve pence).

The teaching of what is true, and the practice of what is good, are the most important objects in domestic life.

R. R. BELLAMY'S
HOUSEHOLD
ALMANACK,
Commercial Advertiser,
AND
YEAR-BOOK OF USEFUL KNOWLEDGE
For 1861,
CONTAINS

A LIST OF FAIRS,
THE RISING AND SETTING OF THE SUN AND MOON;

Golden Maxims for the Household;
A COPIOUS CALENDAR; LAW AND UNIVERSITY TERMS; ECLIPSES; TABLES OF STAMPS AND TAXES, &c.;

Notes on Nursing the Sick;

HINTS FOR HOME HAPPINESS;
OVERCOME THE DIFFICULTIES OF LIFE;
THE USES OF ADVERSITY;

Remarks on the habit of gossip; Consumption and its cause; Valuable Hints in Household Management; How to get on in the World; Useful Receipts; Gardening Operations;

AND OTHER VALUABLE AND IMPORTANT MATTER.

PRICE ONE PENNY.

Burton-upon-Trent:
PRINTED AND PUBLISHED BY R. R. BELLAMY, "WEEKLY NEWS" OFFICE, 25, BRIDGE STREET.

Penny Household Almanacks were a feature in nearly every home. Burton printer and publisher R.R. Bellamy, proprietor of one of the town's early newspapers, has rather cleverly used his cover to advertise just about every example of type that he could set up in his Bridge Street printing shop.

April 15th, 1935
until further notice.

PRICE
ONE PENNY.

Burton Corporation Transport Dept.

MOTOR OMNIBUS SERVICES.

Official Time Tables.

A. B. SLATER, M.Inst.T., *General Manager.*

Another useful 'pennyworth' was the Burton Corporation Transport Department timetable, in this instance for bus services in 1935. Times, fares and stages are all listed, the only journey costing more than 3d being Acorn Inn to Stanton Road terminus, costing 4d. Children over three and under fourteen paid one penny for any distance. It is interesting to find services still indicating the night-time colour light used from tram days to identify routes. For example: Stapenhill-Tutbury Road, green. Buses to Winshill, white. Calais Road-Branston Road, blue. Stanton Road-Acorn Inn, green.

These penny tickets have survived through being left in library books, full value being obtained by subsequent use as bookmarks!

Many years ago an old inhabitant spoke of 'the two best pennyworths in Burton in olden days'. A Stapenhill ferry-boat was operating at least by the fifteenth century. In 1879 over 17,000 people were ferried over the Trent in a two-week period on payment of a penny fare. You then walked across Shipley Meadow to Fleet Green and over the Fleet Stones (later the Fleetstones bridge) to Bond End and town. It was a long walk round over Trent Bridge when the floods were out. In the picture, ferryman Tom Whitley strides purposefully out of Ferry House in the 1880s.

For fifty-three years, until 1940, 'Chippy' Heap's stall stood at the entrance to Burton Market Place, for three generations serving innumerable customers with a pennyworth of chips and peas on an enamel plate. There were immaculate white calico covers around the stall and this carte-de-visite from the 1890s uniquely shows the Heap's handsome horse which hauled the dray on which stall and equipment were carried to and fro, the homeward journey often being around midnight.

Thirteen

Night of the Thirteenth

There was general satisfaction around Linton in 1862 when a new coal field at Coton Park was announced, bringing with it prospects for employment in the area. This pit subsequently became known as Netherseal Colliery, another new mine north of Linton also opening, and becoming Coton Park Colliery.

By 1865 local miners were able to anticipate and afford a relaxing Saturday evening drinking their ale at the Holly Bush Inn, Linton. At around 5 p.m. on Saturday 13 May that year, Matthew Tilley, a collier, went to the inn with Joseph Siddles. At about 6 p.m. a man known as Tom Linney joined the company. His proper name was Thomas Leatherbarrow and he was a professional skate dancer living in Burton. Several times during the evening Linney amused the patrons by dancing on skates. At a later stage Linney arranged to go into an empty house adjoining the inn and announced that Tilley would tie him securely to a chair. This was done in the presence of the inn's customers who then returned to the Holly Bush, leaving the house door closed but unlocked. Within five minutes Linney had walked out of the house loose and his performance was repeated several times.

Later, Linney asked Tilley and Siddles to accompany him down the road saying, 'I will show you a bit of a trick'. They walked about quarter of a mile down the Lullington road until Linney stopped by a tree and said, 'I shall act upon that'. From under his jacket he produced a long rope which he tied round his ankles, thighs and body before throwing the end of the rope over a bough. He then told Tilley to lift him up while Siddles tied the rope taut to a stake in the hedge. As he swung some three or four feet above the ground Tilley asked if he was all right. Linney replied, 'Yes, and if I am not in the Holly Bush before you get there and drink a glass of ale each, I shall forfeit and pay for half a gallon of ale'. Tilley and Siddles then returned to the inn, drank their pints and after ten minutes concluded that Linney had lost his bet and returned down Lullington Road.

The Saturday evening sport was now over. Linney had successfully removed the rope from around ankles, thighs and body but he was still dangling from the tree branch and the rope was tight round his neck.

The following Tuesday saw Tilley and Siddles again at the Holly Bush but this time they were giving a subdued account of Saturday's events for the coroner and his jury. They were followed by Doctor Hall giving medical evidence and then by Thomas Harrad who described himself as a professor of dancing and a performer with ropes, chains and handcuffs practising acts of escapology. He told how he had worked with Linney at the Queen's in Burton and then at the Punch Bowl in Stapenhill. He had later met Linney who told him that subsequently he had persuaded a man to tie him to a tree that night at Stapenhill, eight feet from the ground, and that he had speedily freed himself. 'I told him never to do that again as it was a very dangerous practice', Harrad said, and went on to demonstrate how easily a running noose could have slipped round deceased's neck while freeing himself on that fatal night of the thirteenth. A unanimous verdict was promptly returned – 'Died from accidental strangling'.

Saturday nights at local inns are probably less bizarre today but does anyone fancy a late night stroll down the Lullington road?

The original colliery at Coton Park became Netherseal Colliery when a new mine opened north of Linton and became Coton Park Colliery. Locally it was long referred to as 'Strip an' at it', recalling a lady cutting the first sod and proclaiming 'Right ho, lads, strip an' at it'. Like all South Derbyshire pits it no longer exists. Its sites returned to agricultural use while some other sites have become part of the National Forest.

Main Street, Stapenhill, in the 1920s showing, centre, the original Punch Bowl inn where Tom Linney performed before visiting Linton and from where he 'rehearsed' his escapology act hanging from a local tree. This scene also shows Ball's butchery (left) and the former blacksmith's forge as a small garage with a Pratts petrol pump. Jerrams Lane entrance is beyond the inn, alongside outbuildings of Stapenhill House. Everything past Ball's shop was soon to be demolished and replaced by the present Punch Bowl and Stapenhill Gardens.

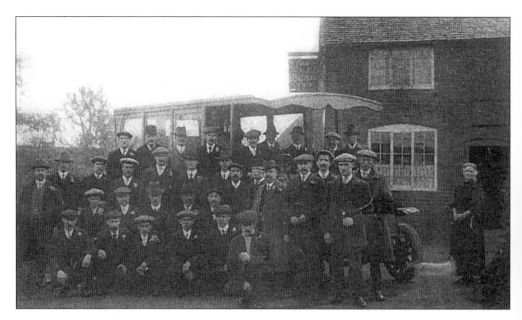

You can still visit the Holly Bush inn at Linton where Tom Linney performed his skate dancing and from where he staged his last 'trick' in 1865. This scene outside the Holly Bush can also be dated to around 1920, but while the inn had probably changed little, much had altered in sixty years. Linney had walked out from Burton but the inn's customers are now believed to be embarking on a bus trip to Chatsworth.

The Holly Bush inn is at the end of Linton's High Street with the road continuing towards Lullington. This view is no longer recognisable today but the image from around 1900 almost certainly depicts the High Street that Tom Linney saw as he walked up to the inn on that fateful May evening in 1865.

Fourteen

Not-so-good Old Days

At the start of the eighteenth century poor folk of Burton on parish relief had to wear a distinctive cloth badge, a humiliating and much resented practice. In 1728 a workhouse was established in a converted barn in Anderstaff Lane (Wetmore) which served to house the town's poor until a new building was erected in 1838 in Horninglow Street. This catered for 300 paupers until, in 1884, Belvedere House was built. The former workhouse was then used by various firms, for storage.

When built, Belvedere House was surrounded by fields, the area not being developed for housing until around 1900. Although Belvedere had facilities for different classes of inmates and was a great improvement on earlier provision, some typical poor law features persisted into the twentieth century. We can understand how impoverished elderly couples dreaded 'the shadow of the workhouse' – removed there when finally unable to fend for themselves, they were still told they could see each other twice a week! The position was eased after the first old age pensions were introduced in 1908. The practices of stone breaking and oakum picking (untwisting old ropes), more associated with prisons, still continued in use for the able bodied.

Whatever faults the workhouse may have had, its inmates were better off than many who transgressed outside. In 1862 George Baker stole two loaves of bread, value one penny each, and was sentenced to a month at the House of Correction with hard labour. In 1866, 'a miserable looking man who could not or would not speak' was charged under the Vagrancy Act with sleeping in Mr. Outram's ash pit. He was committed to prison for fourteen days with hard labour. And when Mr. M.T. Bass was supporting the tightening of game laws in the Night Poaching Bill (1862) he reported that there were 100 people in Burton with no ostensible means of living but by night poaching and that the police claimed 3,000 were similarly engaged within the county.

Belvedere House included an infirmary, school and casual wards for vagrants. As the century progressed support for poverty became more humane and with charitable help, much outdoor assistance was also given (averaging over 1,500 paupers in Edwardian days) while there was an average of 550 inmates. Administration was in the hands of the Burton Union Board supported by locally elected guardians including clergymen and representatives of charitable bodies who made valuable contributions, financial and administrative.

With the establishment of the National Health Service from 1948, Belvedere House was upgraded and incorporated as part of Burton Infirmary. Maternity units were transferred there with other departments following. Any stigma attached to the name of the former workhouse led to the new development being named the Andressey Hospital. From that beginning came the final switch of all hospital provision from the old infirmary site to the large new Queen's Hospital of today.

This photograph, dated 1911, includes the master and matron of the workhouse and the staff members of the Burton Union Board, the chaplain, medical officer, and possibly others associated with administration or charitable assistance. Denis Stuart's *County Borough History* disclosed that in addition to the average of 550 paupers during 1911, 145 lunatics and fifty-seven vagrants were on the books, food and necessities costing over £4,800. A Ladies Visiting Committee contributed greatly through charitable work on behalf of the Union Board.

There is recollection of the workhouse children having short cut hair; girls and infants wearing pinafores; boys in black with stiff white collars; and all with highly polished black boots. This is confirmed in the scene of around 1904. The lady, seated left in the previous photograph, was presumably the children's matron as she appears here, a little younger. Some children were sent to residential homes or orphanages. Girls often became domestic servants; boys went for sea training or became errand boys or farm workers. Some older children went overseas as emigrants. Spectators watch from Belvedere/Calais Road corner.

Belvedere Rd. Burton-on-Trent.

These Belvedere Road houses were recently built when this card was posted in 1909. The 1900 Ordnance Survey map shows the road running through fields with only Lower Outwoods Farm as an isolated dwelling. Calais Road was also developed about this time. The view shows Belvedere House with its landmark chimney and clock tower, the latter dominating the scene until the newly-named Andressey Hospital had replaced most of the old workhouse complex.

A political reflection of the times. Important social developments came about with the Old Age Pensions Act of 1908 and the National Insurance Act of 1911. The pension was five shillings a week (25p) at seventy provided any other income was less than ten shillings (50p). Adoption caused a storm because of the cost! Lloyd-George was the central figure in these Liberal provisions and this card recalls the exhortations against Britain becoming 'a servile nation of stamp lickers'.

THE STAMP THAT WANTS A LOT OF LICKING

AND THE MAN

107

There is a certain pathos about this Lawson Wood advertising card of 1920 used by Johnson Brothers (Dyers), whose local shop was at 7 Station Street. There were many vagrants between the wars, some of them, sadly, unemployed servicemen discharged after 1918 and they moved around calling at local workhouse casual wards. Wards at Burton and Tamworth closed from 31 October 1940 and relief was no longer available to the casual poor. The nearest wards then still open were at Basford, Stafford, Wolverhampton and Birmingham.

This postcard shows 'Relief of the Poor at Mount St Bernard's Abbey' (Leicestershire) in 1907, a reminder that during the long history of Burton Abbey, the almoner and his lay assistants would have responsibility for care of the local poor and needy. Dissolution of the abbey (1540) resulted in responsibility for the parish poor passing to local communities, ultimately leading to the workhouse provisions outlined in this chapter. Perhaps some of these men tramped the seventeen or so miles between Mount St Bernard's and Burton casual ward.

Fifteen
A District Miscellany

This final chapter comprises a very varied collection of scenes and memorabilia – a mixed miscellany of items, not fitting easily into any other chapter, but contributing to this book's portrayal of life, events and social history around the district in days gone by.

Certain railway lines attracted postcard publishers who used a standard cartoon with appropriate local caption. This is Reg Carter's drawing, complementing 'Tutbury Jenny' (sic) 'Our Local Express' by Cynicus with a donkey pulling an ancient engine. Last trains when lines finally closed were often quite dignified affairs but the last run of Tutbury Jenny on 11 June 1960 was a lively, robust occasion, hundreds of passengers noisily commemorating the event.

A rather disturbing picture from times before controversy over hunting. As well as the area's fox hunting, J.S. Simnett produced a pictorial record of otter hounds at work, a seasonal sport around Tutbury on the Dove and its streams. He inscribed this scene 'The Kill' and it also shows keen spectators, male and female. The luckless otter has disappeared from local rivers, mainly through being hunted, with pollution perhaps a later factor. Preservation of fishing stock was claimed as justification for this activity.

It is hard to associate this view of Old Road, Branston, with today's avenue of modern housing. As seen from Main Street, c. 1930, it is a rural lane with cottages of character. Land on the right was once a reed bed but is remembered from the 1960s as becoming a tip for builders' rubble. Development soon followed, however, with the loss of trees and roadside greenery so that little of the Old Road remains.

Now beyond living memory, but not forgotten, was the distress caused by the miner's strike of 1912. The Miners' Federation sought an eight hour day (achieved 1908) and a minimum or 'living' wage and it was this that precipitated the 1912 closure of virtually every colliery. When miners were on piece-work, earnings depended on conditions in individual pits. Many South Derbyshire miners (some 4,000 involved locally) and their families faced poverty while coal shortages meant workers in other industries, such as potters and brickmakers, also became unemployed. A miner's strike pay was ten shillings (50p) a week. During the strike, miners dug for coal in gardens, outcrops and on spoil heaps. A close vote ended action in April but the new local minimum wage was $32\frac{1}{2}$p per day, well short of the demand for 40p (eight shillings) to meet the call for 'eight hours work, eight hours play, eight hours sleep, eight bob a day'. (eight 'bob' being eight shillings).

The main A38 at Barton Turns (or more correctly, Barton Turnings, being the point where barges were turned after using the adjoining canal wharf). Roads often used to be lined with telegraph poles and, with little traffic, one could hear the wires humming. The garage (left) was opposite the former Vine Inn (now known as the Barton Turns Inn) and was a long narrow structure tucked in between road and canal, its site surviving as a car park. On the right is the former Railway Inn, often locally called the Flying Horse, presumably a reference to steam engines on the nearby main line. In the 1950s this length of the A38 became a cul-de-sac with a new section of road curving round behind the houses and now incorporated into today's A38 dual carriageway.

A splendid period piece from Barton under Needwood – an enlargement of a Victorian *carte-de-visite*, the pictorial ancestor of the picture postcard. Radhurst Grange on Main Street was built around 1760, and around the time of this photograph was the private 'Middle Class school' conducted by Mr Holdsworth (University of London) who had seven boarders (plus seevn children of his own). Most interesting however is the steam-ploughing engine, an early example of mechanised farming. Usually provided by contractors, a pair of engines would be needed for ploughshares and they could also be used for threshing. Here the balance plough has four shares on each side (both sets raised for road travel). One engine would be positioned each side of a field and the plough would be drawn across by cables from the drum under the engine. The ploughshares not in use would be swung clear and then lowered, to be hauled back by the second engine for the next set of furrows to be ploughed.

A water carnival was a feature of many Burton galas and riverside events. Against a background of fireworks a procession of decorated and illuminated boats followed a circular course on the Trent. Images produced during the evening parade tend to be rather dark but this photograph, taken earlier from the rowing club landing stages, gives a good impression of the elaborate decoration of participating craft at one of the events from between the wars.

In 1911, Burton had a new bridge over at least part of the Trent. This plank pontoon bridge was erected by the Territorials under Lt J. Slack and Sgt Wain on the occasion of Burton Flower Show on 30/31 August. It connected the Hay and the Broadholme, to which admission was one shilling (5p) via Trent Bridge, entrances illuminated by the Corporation gas department. There was again an extensive programme of events including cricket, water carnival, fireworks and illuminations on Stapenhill Riverside Walk.

THE MAYOR.
The Most Hon. The Marquess of Anglesey.

THE MAYORESS.
Lady Alexander Paget.

Prizes at the 1911 Flower Show were presented by Lady Alexander Paget who, from November 1911, served as Mayoress when her son, the sixth Marquess of Anglesey, became Burton's Mayor. The Marquess undertook this public office after some local criticism as an absent landlord, large parts of Burton still being part of the Anglesey estates. The Marquess married Lady Victoria Manners, a daughter of the Duke of Rutland, in 1912. Lady Alexander, his mother, was the widow of Lord Alexander Victor Paget.

Scouts and Guides were immensely popular organizations in the early years of the century and they were prominent participants at any public event or in processions. This delightful period group was posed at a scout camp at Hoar Cross on August Bank Holiday 1913, although you do have to look hard to spot any scouts! It was actually a day for visitors to look in on the camp and proud and interested families have certainly shown their support.

Rimless Glasses
fitted as we fit them are
Elegance Itself

Two scenes of feminine elegance used for advertising purposes in the early twentieth century. That for rimless glasses was sent out by Mr A. Brooks, the Burton optician, at 38 Station Street in 1917 advising a client that new glasses were ready for collection. Similar rimless glasses have again come back into fashion.

The Burton Opera House publicity postcard dates from 1913 and reproduces a high quality theatre poster of the period when leading artists were frequently commissioned, in this instance, L. Barribal. The Opera House was often designated simply as 'The Theatre' on this type of publicity, with 'The New Theatre' and, (particularly for variety shows), 'The Hippodrome' also used.

THE ~ THEATRE, Burton ~ on ~ Trent.
Monday, November 10th, Six Nights
Matinee Saturday at 2.30

The Girl in the Train

116

The 1900 Burton directory lists over fifty private butchers. At 213 Waterloo Street on Albert Street corner, was the shop of J. Loynes (later Mrs Alice Loynes). This is probably a posed display for Abrahams to photograph but it was quite usual for meat and poultry to hang outside in defiance of dust and flies, although Loynes advertised that meat was kept in a cold chamber in hot weather. They also had Market Hall premises and proudly stressed that they supplied English meat only.

The first purpose-built department store (as distinct from shops that expanded) was the Bon Marché in Brixton. This name became a popular choice for small provincial shops selling a selection of fancy goods, toys, etc. Burton's Bon Marché was at 48 Station Street, the premises still surviving. With an even cheaper range of items were little shops and market stalls known as bazaars, such as Piper's Penny Bazaar, also in Station Street. The pattern continued with the arrival of Woolworth's Threepenny and Sixpenny Stores in the 1920s.

Always Something New at the **BON MARCHE.**

INSTRUCTIVE AND AMUSING TOYS.

GAMES FOR WINTER EVENINGS in Great Variety

CREST CHINA, PICTURE POSTCARDS, DOLLS, FANCY GLASS & CHINA. BAGS, PURSES, &c.

Popular Prices. Inspection Invited.

48 Station Street, Burton.

A. BERNARD, Proprietor.

No subsequent photograph of Dove Bridge at Tutbury shows it to greater advantage than this engraving of 1832, published by W. Hodson of Tutbury, and recorded just seventeen years after its construction. Staffordshire and Derbyshire shared the £8,000 cost equally. It replaced an earlier bridge of around 1420, which was situated a little way upstream. One suspects that the artist has omitted some features and foliage in order to highlight the castle and the church.

The New Trent Bridge, Burton-on-Trent

A traffic-free view of Trent Bridge after the widening of 1924/26, showing the railings and boarding which protected pavements until removed in the Second World War. Even in the 1920s there was still sufficient horse traffic for vehicles to spatter manure over luckless pedestrians and the scene shows evidence of this, the tramlines often obliging vehicles to travel close to the path. An interesting half-hour census in 1913 recorded forty-seven horse vehicles and 118 pedestrians. (There were seven trams, seven cars, two motorcycles, five handcarts and three prams!).

Dove Cliff Hall, Stretton (c. 1790), now a hotel, has many local associations. The Thornewills were iron forgers in New Street and at Clay Mills from the eighteenth century. In 1869 Michael Arthur Bass (later Lord Burton) married Harriet Georgina Thornewill; her sister and companion, Miss Jane Thornewill, becoming noted as one of King Edward VII's bridge partners. It then became the Charrington's residence, their brewery being in Abbey Street from 1872 to 1926. Later it was the Sharp family home where Geoffrey Sharp staged outdoor Shakespeare and rehearsed his spectacular revue 'Midsummer Madness', celebrating the Queen's Coronation in 1953. Old Stretton recollections have included references to a cockpit and cockfights, which continued after they were declared illegal. In contrast, the Charringtons welcomed the annual Stretton Sunday School treat, participants marching in procession behind a band, the very young and the elderly in horse-drawn drays from the brewery.

Today's fly-over makes it hard to realise that until the 1960s this was where the road from Stretton joined the main A38 at Clay Mills, a simple T-junction alongside a picturesque old cottage.

In 1919 the National Council of Social Service was formed (subsequently the National Council for Voluntary Organisations). It aimed to encourage village community activities. A postcard dated 15 May 1935 adds to the sparse record of Kingstanding, an isolated country house not well documented. The message reads: 'Here is an aerial view of the training centre where I am taking two courses of three weeks; instruction in the various crafts as practised in our social centres is given us during our stay'.

Looking down from the Bass water tower (c. 1906) the photographer has panned the view between Andressey Bridge and the Parish church, overlooking the former Worthington malthouses on the present library site. Beyond, the Ice Cold Storage stands out along with the chimneys of the Corporation yard and refuse destructor plant. Ferry Bridge crosses (top left), but estate building at Stapenhill and Drakelow power station are developments for the future, a secluded Trent valley stretching away into the distance.

Research for particular topics sometimes brings to notice unexpected, strange or amusing items of local interest. Retaining a note of them can build up a fascinating little collection of the odd, the bizarre and the eccentric. One chance discovery revealed that on 15 July 1865 all the printers employed at Burton's printing establishments (Bellamy's, Darley's, Wesley's and Whitehurst's) assembled at the railway station to proceed to Hanbury for their first-ever Wayzegoose dinner, to be served by Thomas Foster at the Shoulder of Mutton inn.

In passing one might reflect that to head for Hanbury by rail must have involved something of an uphill trek after leaving the train, possibly at Scropton, which had a station until 1872.

However, the occasion was reviving a curious old custom, probably of seventeenth century origin, whereby printing employees gathered for a meal of goose. The obsolete word *wase* meant a bundle of stubble, hence wasegoose (waysgoose or wayzgoose) was a 'fat stubble-fed goose'. A scratch cricket match followed and 'three fire balloons caused great excitement'. An excellent dinner, hearty toasts and capital singing made for a 'most enjoyable excursion' but we find no contemporary record of the occasion being repeated. By way of illustration, an interesting survival from Hanbury's past, dates back over 200 years.

SERVIRE CHRISTO EST REGNARE

Rev.ᵈ Hugh Bailye, A.M.

Hanbury, Staffordshire.

This is the tower of St Werburgh's church, Hanbury as it appeared at the end of the eighteenth century (*c.* 1783) when Revd. Hugh Bailye was vicar and had this steel engraving made for his personal bookplate. A gentlemen with a library would insert one of these in the front of valued books to indicate ownership. The vicar's handsome example is also of historic interest because in 1842 the upper section of the tower became unsafe and was rebuilt; the top section was then further altered in 1890.

Found backing a local picture, two photographs of polo players were put aside until it emerged that Barton had 'polo fields' where John Taylor school now stands and where the game was played in late Victorian times. Why a sport otherwise unrecorded for this area was practised at Barton may be explained by the number of retired army officers residing locally. Old maps almost certainly confirm the location of this unique pictorial record. The background track-way was probably part of the 'lost' Hall Lane, which gave access to the rear of Barton Hall where General Fowler-Butler lived. Accounts from the 1880s and up to 1911 indicate athletic or sports meetings on the polo field or polo ground. The earlier occasions acknowledge the Polo Club and it is known that visiting teams came to Barton to play matches.

The game of water polo reputedly had its origins in Burton. Played at the Corporation Baths, it enjoyed a period of great popularity in the early twentieth century, and was played until the baths closed.

Those who know Ashfield House today may find difficulty in reconciling it with this photograph from around 1900, when it was the residence of J.R. Morris, four times mayor of Burton and owner of one of the town's biggest cooperages. There have been alterations and extensions but the original house is still quite recognisable. The view over the town has been further restricted by new building; and these thickly planted grounds now include a bowling green and car parking.

Now nationally known as an elegant health spa resort, Hoar Cross Hall here displays the elegance of an earlier era when it was the private residence of the Meynells. This crowded Edwardian room was typical of its day and the view is one of a series of both interior and garden scenes taken by Simnett recording the Hoar Cross Hall of those times.

Burton breweries were always to the fore with original advertising and one very successful innovation was the introduction of 'bottle' vehicles. Worthingtons led the way as early as 1906 with this specially built 40hp Napier advertising India Pale Ale. It featured at the Brewers' Exhibition of that year before its publicity travels, but unfortunately the card does not identify which White Horse Hotel forms the background.

Allsopp's pale ale bottle stands upright as a horse-drawn display, obviously designed principally for use on show grounds. Again there is no clue to the location of this fine photograph but the large crowds suggest a major county or agricultural show.

A group photograph of 1935 taken at the annual meeting of Marston's brewery agents with S.H. Evershed (Senior) in the front row wearing a light suit. His son, S.H. Evershed, became managing director in that year. Marstons, fiercely independent at this time, had expanded through a succession of mergers and this large gathering of agents assembled from many parts of the country.

Although appearing twenty years ago in our earliest collection, it seemed appropriate, in view of the Bass Museum's Silver Jubilee, to recall Bass engine No. 9 and the directors' saloon 'in steam' on the company's extensive private railway system. No. 9 was a 1901 replacement for an earlier engine and returned to the Bass Museum in 1977 after being preserved at the County Museum, Shugborough. The coach conveyed King Edward VII in 1902 and was used for inspections and for conveying visitors round the brewery.

The saying 'to take the cake' (or biscuit) means 'that beats everything' or 'carries off the prize'. The reference is to a traditional cake-walk, when competitors circled a cake in pairs, the judges choosing the couple who walked most gracefully. In the early twentieth century it developed into a popular dance. G.H. Chirgwin was a popular music hall singer but we can't spot him hidden in the picture. Wallace's Burton shop closed in the early 1900s.

Photographs of 'lost' streets are scarce but this is St Paul's Street East, a narrow roadway of small houses, shops and the Railway Inn, incongruously dwarfed by Burton Town Hall, directly opposite. After King Edward's visit in 1902 this unsatisfactory frontage for Lord Burton's gift to the town led to all domestic buildings being cleared and King Edward Place laid out. Here the crowd awaits the return of the Burton Boer War Volunteers from the thanksgiving service for a lunch served in the town hall.

Very much a recollection of changing times and attitudes, this item from around 1930 reflects moves from property rental to home ownership. It is all very different from today's high-powered housing market with the Halifax advertising their small local branch in the offices of Thomas Shelley & Son, an old-established firm (1881) of house and insurance agents, auctioneers and valuers at 55 Station Street. This was opposite George Street and adjoined the entrance to Bass's New Brewery, an area now completely swept away.

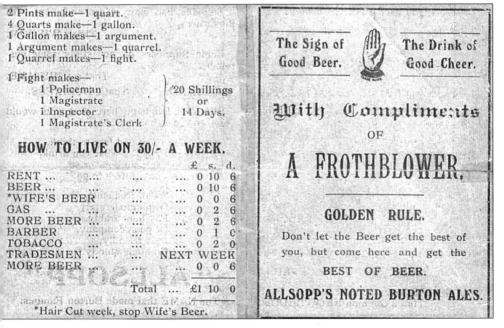
Part of an amusing little publicity item from Allsopp's brewery issued in days when thirty shillings a week (£1.50) was an average wage. There were certain aspects of social history contained within the 'budget' such as typical rent and gas charges, but there are probably instances where the humour veils a near truth in respect of other headings.

What more appropriate image to conclude this volume – a splendid group of Burton maltsters. Between them they have all the essential requirements for their work – the malt shovels, ploughing sticks, rakes and, most important of all, quantities of ale. How wonderful if this group could only assemble to look upon the town's controversial representation of a malt shovel. If we could then ask for their comments what a dramatic final page this might have been – if printable!

Things present are judged by things past.

(Sixteenth-century proverb)

Acknowledgements

For this latest anthology of Burton upon Trent and district, we have again largely drawn upon our own collected material. We are, as always, indebted to those photographers, known and unknown, whose images make such a volume possible. In addition we owe thanks to many people who have been of assistance in various ways – in providing or loaning illusive scenes or for additional information or for identification of people and places. In particular we thank Mrs Margaret Brenan, Rose-Marie Davies, Steve Gardner, Mrs Pat Gilman, Mrs Jessica Griffiths, Tim Jeffcoat, Neville Ingley, Mrs Rosalind Stonier, Ernie Sutton, and P.M. White. We are again indebted to Michelle Farman for preparing the text for publication. We acknowledge help from Burton upon Trent Public Library and from the files of the *Burton Daily Mail*.

The authors dedicate this volume to the memory of the late Denis Stuart, in recognition of his many contributions to local history and recalling a long and happy association.

Reference to the Bretby 'counsel of the neighbourhood' is based on an account in *England Under Henry III* by Margaret Hennings.

This new selection of old photographs and
postcards follows the success of several previous
Burton upon Trent and East Staffordshire books by
local authors Geoffrey Sowerby and Richard Farman.
Like *Tales of the Town* and *Looking Back*, also in the
Images of England series, *Burton upon Trent
Recollections* combines rare archive material with a
wealth of fascinating local information to evoke a
past way of life in this historic town. The many
previously unpublished photographs are
supplemented by advertisements, wartime campaign
leaflets, certificates and newspaper cuttings dating
back over a hundred years, all of which are sure to
stir memories and stimulate nostalgia among Burton's
older residents.

Special occasions and events are recalled here, but
so too are the everyday lives of the people of Burton,
making this an important historical record as well as
a collection that will delight all those who know
Burton upon Trent.

Images *of England*
is part of the *Archive Photographs* series

Tempus Publishing Limited
The Mill, Brimscombe Port,
Stroud, Gloucestershire, GL5 2QG

£11.99

A–Z
OF
EASTBOURNE

PLACES - PEOPLE - HISTORY

KEVIN GORDON